Understanding Compression
Data Compression for Modern Developers

Colt McAnlis and Aleks Haecky

Beijing · Boston · Farnham · Sebastopol · Tokyo

Understanding Compression

by Colt McAnlis and Aleks Haecky

Printed in the United States of America.

Published by O'Reilly Media, Inc., 1005 Gravenstein Highway North, Sebastopol, CA 95472.

O'Reilly books may be purchased for educational, business, or sales promotional use. Online editions are also available for most titles (*http://safaribooksonline.com*). For more information, contact our corporate/institutional sales department: 800-998-9938 or *corporate@oreilly.com*.

Editor: Tim McGovern	**Indexer:** Ellen Troutman-Zaig
Production Editor: Melanie Yarbrough	**Interior Designer:** David Futato
Copyeditor: Octal Publishing, Inc.	**Cover Designer:** Karen Montgomery
Proofreader: Jasmine Kwityn	**Illustrator:** Melanie Yarbrough

July 2016:   First Edition

Revision History for the First Edition

2016-07-11:   First Release

See *http://oreilly.com/catalog/errata.csp?isbn=9781491961537* for release details.

978-1-491-96153-7

[LSI]

From CLM

To JAM and MLM: I swear to Zuul, that if you don't eat your broccoli right now, I'm going to write a book. And in the dedication of that book, I'm going to call you out as being afraid of a piece of foliage that humans have been eating for thousands of generations. Then, 20 years from now, when you have kids of your own, I'm going to pull that book out, and show you what I wrote, and laugh in your face, because you'll know how crazy you're making me right now. #parenting

To KMKM: How about another decade, just for good measure?

From AH

To AHS and GHS: I hoped you'd learn to cook. Instead, you proved that humankind can survive on fresh apples and stale supermarket sushi.

Table of Contents

Table of Contents

Foreword

When I first began programming, I had no idea what data compression was nor why it mattered. Luckily, my Apple II Plus computer came with 0.000048 GB of memory (48 KB), which was quite a lot in 1979, and was enough to let me explore programming and computer graphics without realizing that my programs and data were constantly being compressed and decompressed behind the scenes in order to reduce their size in memory. Thanks, Woz!

After programming for a few years, I had discovered:

- Data compression took time and could slow down my software.
- Changing my data organization could make the compressed data smaller.
- There are a bewildering variety of complicated data compression algorithms.

This led to the realization that compression was not a rigid black box; rather, it's a flexible tool that greatly influenced the quality of my software and could be manipulated in several ways:

- Changing compression algorithms could make my software run faster.
- Pairing my data organization with the right compression algorithm could make my data smaller.
- Choosing the wrong data organization or algorithm could make my data larger (and/or run slower).

Ah! Now I knew why data compression mattered. If things weren't fitting into memory or were decompressing too slowly, I could slightly change my data organization to better fit the compression algorithm. I'd simply put numbers together in one group, strings in another, build tables of recurring data types, or truncate fractions into integers. I didn't need to do the hard work of evaluating and adopting new compression algorithms if I could fit my data to the algorithm.

Then, I began making video games professionally, and most of the game data was created by not-so-technical artists, designers, and musicians. It turned out that math was not their favorite topic of discussion, and they were less than excited about changing the game data so that it would take advantage of my single go-to compression algorithm. Well, if the data organization couldn't be improved, that left choosing the best compression algorithm to pair up with all of this great artistic data.

I surveyed the various compression algorithms and found there were a couple of broad categories suitable for my video game data:

Lossless
- De-duplication (LZ)
- Entropy (Huffman, Arithmetic)

Lossy
- Reduced precision (truncation or decimation)
- Image/video
- Audio

For text strings and binary data, I used LZ to compress away repeating duplicate data patterns. Pixel data went through lossy vector quantization (VQ) to map pixels to a color palette. Audio data went through lossy decimation and linear predictive coding (LPC) to reduce the bits per second. The output of any of those compressors could then go into a lossless Huffman compressor for additional statistical entropy compression, if the CPU was fast enough.

During the 1980s and 1990s, I worked on about 30 games, most of which used these compression algorithms along with simple data build tools that performed limited optimizations of the data organization.

But then, around the year 2000, the situation became more complex. There is an ongoing arms race between data generation tools and data display and analysis. The consequences have been software performance, storage size, network congestion, and the efficient pairing of compression algorithms with data organization.

This data flood has been partially offset by larger storage (Blu-ray discs, terabyte hard drives, cloud storage), faster multicore CPUs, new lossless compression algorithms such as BWT, ANS, and PAQ, as well as dramatic improvements in lossy codecs for image, video, and audio data. However, data sizes are growing faster each year and dwarf the slow improvements in network bandwidth, compression algorithm improvements, and storage capacity.

Which brings us to the present and why this book matters.

How can a programmer learn which algorithms to use on their data and which data changes will help or hinder a particular algorithm? What would really help is an overview of the major data compression algorithms to guide developers through the myriad choices now available. Most developers don't need to wade through all the theory and math details required to implement these algorithms; instead, they need a road map of the strengths and weaknesses of these algorithms, and how to take advantage of them for specific use cases.

I've greatly enjoyed implementing, using, and watching the evolution of data compression algorithms over the past 37 years. I hope this book will help demystify data compression and provide a starting point for software engineers to learn about compression algorithms and help them make better software.

— *John Brooks, CTO, Blue Shift, Inc.*

Preface

Data compression is everywhere, and it's as utterly essential for modern computing as it was, when one megabyte was a lot, and data was transferred in kilobits per second. In a sense, we have come full circle, from antique computers with limited memory and bandwidth, to mobile devices with limited memory and costly data plans.

Fortunately, there are tools, APIs, and packages that can compress your data for you. Understanding how they work will help you to choose the *right* compression for your data, which will directly translate into happier users, cost savings, and more revenue for you.

Data compression is built on math, and let's face it, for most mere mortals, math is hard. Like, *really* hard. Like, it used to be one of the hardest things about being a programmer. Imagine Claude Shannon, the father of data compression, who was really good at math, hacking away at some chalkboard, scribbling rows and rows of crazy complex equations.

What's even more crazy, is that modern programmers don't really need to know math. Any eight-year-old kid in the world can jump online, work through a tutorial, and publish their own web page or application before even enrolling in Algebra class.

And this is, we believe, why the field of data compression has been stagnant over the past 20 years. Despite the fact that two billion[1] people are on mobile devices and regularly experience problems with memory capacity and poor Internet connectivity, data compression remains a semi-stagnant computational technology. Because programmers don't know math.

Because math is hard.

---

[1] This is the number as of 2015. If you're reading this book some time in the future, it will be different. Also, thanks for reading the book! Also, how did you survive the robo-apocalypse?

You see, compression isn't really about data. The early founders of data compression weren't thinking about data. They were thinking about statistics. They were looking for, and found, different ways to manipulate the *probability distributions* of symbols in data sets, and exploit those trends to produce smaller data sets that contained the same information.

As computing became more common and less mathematical, the average programmer needed to know less and less about statistics and other advanced math. And so, despite the early 2000s bringing the largest technology boom in computing history, data compression has had maybe two or three advances *in its entire scientific field*.

Because compression is hard.

Because it's built on math.

Now, let's be fair and practical here. Today, most programmers and content developers don't need to know advanced math or understand how compression works, because they can just grab a decent data compression library, throw their data at it, and ship it out into the wild-blue yonder.

However, moving forward, this is not going to be enough. Predictions are that by 2025, five *billion* humans will be using computers and transferring data over the Internet. Considering that data production has gone through the roof, we're about to have too much data, with carriers that can't transfer it fast enough, and data warehouses too small to hold it all. Of course, one solution is faster, better compression, using innovative algorithms that have yet to be invented.

Using math.

Which is hard.

The other solution is to teach anyone who will listen how compression works. So, instead of grabbing some random compression tool, you can choose the very best compression and get your data to your users in the most efficient manner.

That's where this book comes from. It's an attempt to minimize the vast, enormous craziness that is the science of data compression, and reduce it to something that mere mortals can understand and apply to their daily data needs. We will try to explain the fundamentals of data compression with tables, diagrams, and data flows—and as little math as possible. Much like Colt's YouTube video series Compressor Head (*https://g.co/compressorhead*), this book hopes to teach compression to pretty much anybody who's survived high school—even if you're not a programmer.

But let's be honest: if you want to really understand this stuff, you'll need to do the mental gymnastics. Compression, like riding a bicycle, is difficult until your mind goes "grok," and then it all makes perfect sense. But you must stick it out and work through the examples to get there.

Just to be clear, our goal is not to make you a compression expert. That would require pretty heavy mathematics (which is hard!). Our goal is to make you understand compression *algorithms*. Sometimes, this will mean using the proper terminology; sometimes it will mean using wrong but far more descriptive terminology. We're not trying to prepare you for water-cooler conversations with other compression folk. We want to give you enough information that you can make the right business decisions about compression.

Finally, and honestly, data compression is also really *cool*. Well, we think so, and we hope that you'll think so, too, as you are delving into this book.

We had fun writing this book, and we hope you'll have fun digging into the science of data compression.

How to Read This Book

Like any good story, this book answers all the *W* questions. *What* is data compression and *why* do you want to know about it? *When* was data compression invented? *Who* are the people who dedicated their lives to eliminating a few more bits? *Where* in your product development cycles should you care about the size of your data? And most importantly, *how* does it all work to save you bits, money, and your user's data plans?

This being an actual, printed volume of pages organized in chronological order, we strongly suggest you start at the beginning and work your way through each chapter. You see, each chapter builds on the previous chapter, not just historically, but also introducing terminology and evolving algorithms. We built the book to be read in an orderly fashion, and the easiest way through the material is to follow that path.

How to Read This Book Backwards

If you are the kind of person whose eyes sparkle more at the sight of money than intricate algorithms, you may read this book backwards. Let yourself be thoroughly convinced that data compression is the most amazing thing since sliced bread (with butter!), and then, energized by those convictions, tackle the work of understanding how compression actually works (because understanding it will result in, you guessed it, more money). Ready?

Chapter Synopsis

Let's face it, chapter synopsis chapters are boring, and we promised you that, like William Goldman in The Princess Bride, we'd stick with just the juicy bits. So, while we ask you not to skip chapter two, feel free to skip this synopsis. Skim the table of contents to find out about, well, the contents of this book, or just go ahead and read the book since you are already holding it in your hands. But if you want to dip your toes into the topic before taking the plunge, here is a little warning on what you are getting yourself into.

Chapter 1, Let's Not Be Boring

In this chapter we tell you everything you need to know if you don't have time to actually read this book. We can divide compression algorithms into five buckets: variable-length codes, statistical compression, dictionary encodings, context modeling, and multi-context modeling. Claude Shannon invented a way of measuring the information content of a message and called it Information Entropy. The whole point of compression is to encode data using fewest possible symbols into the fewest possible bits. The foundation of the whole internet is data compression. You should compress all your data. That's it. You can stop reading now.

Chapter 2, Do Not Skip This Chapter

Don't skip this chapter because it lays out the fundamentals, such as how to represent the whole world in zeros and ones, an introduction to Information Theory, and Entropy as the Minimum Bits Needed to Represent a Number.

Chapter 3, Breaking Entropy

According to Claude Shannon, Entropy puts a limit on how small you can make a data set. Compression is all about breaking this limit by exploiting two properties of real data: ordering and relationships between symbols.

Chapter 4, Variable-Length Codes

You'll learn how to string together 0s and 1s to make unique, variable length codewords, and then assign the shortest ones to the most probable symbols in the dataset. And you'll meet Peter Elias.

Chapter 5, Statistical Encoding

One size never fits all, and statistical encoders create custom VLCs that are optimized for particular datasets. You'll build a Huffman tree using sticky notes, explore arithmetic coding, and meet Jarek Duda who usurped them both by introducing arithmetic numerical systems.

Chapter 6, Adaptive Statistical Encoding

Real data streams change, and adaptive encoders optimize themselves according to the local properties of the data they are processing.

Let's Not Be Boring

Welcome to the first chapter of a book about a niche section of computing. We're supposed to set the stage here for the entire book (that's what the publisher says), and really hook the reader (that would be you). We're expected to talk about history, a handful of basics, and anything else that we can do to try and ease you into the topic of compression as gently (but interestingly) as possible. Without math. Because math is hard.[1]

But let's be real, that's boring for you to read, and for us to write.

So here's what we're going to do, instead. This book is about compression. And compression is all about the most compact representation of data. So, we're going to run through this introductory stuff in the shortest, most compressed form possible.

First, we're going to talk about buckets. Then, we're going to introduce you to this rebel named Claude Shannon, who pretty much ruined our life while simultaneously creating every important thing that you love about computers. Finally, we are going to reveal to you the one essential thing you need to know about data compression. And without going out of our way (hardly!), we'll make clear how compression pays off in better, cheaper, and faster apps.

Do we have a deal?

The Five Buckets of Compression Algorithms

Data compression algorithms are a really, really big space. Fortunately, these algorithms fall into a few buckets, which makes things a lot easier to understand. To

---

1 Yep, that's the last time we'll say this.

throw the words at you, they are *variable-length codes, statistical compression, dictionary encodings, context modeling,* and *multicontext modeling*. Each of these five high-level buckets contains a horde of algorithm variations, which is a good thing; each variation differs slightly in intended input data, performance, memory constraints, and output sizes. Picking the correct variant means carrying out tests on your data and the *encoders* to find the one that works best.

Now, you can use these buckets together, because some buckets contain algorithms whose entire purpose is to transform the data so that another bucket can be more efficient at compressing it.

For you to be viewed as a compression guru, you need to understand the buckets, how they fit together, and what types of variants to use from which bucket for your own data sets.

Let's get started.

Claude Shannon Is Infuriating!

Back in the 1940s, a statistical researcher named Claude Shannon published several papers detailing research he did while working in the military during World War II, and later at Bell Labs.

Claude was a pretty smart guy (and very good at math). Before he left the University of Michigan in 1936, he'd racked up bachelor's degrees in engineering and mathematics. He then went on to do a bunch of crazy post-graduate stuff at the Massachusetts Institute of Technology, and his master's thesis, "A Symbolic Analysis of Relay and Switching Circuits" (*https://www.cs.virginia.edu/~evans/greatworks/shannon38.pdf*), became the foundation of modern electrical switch-based computing.

In 1948, Shannon published *A Mathematical Theory of Communication* (*http://bit.ly/28OvyFH*), which detailed how to best encode information that a sender wants to transmit, thus inventing the entire field of *Information Theory*. Messages can be encoded in many ways—think "alphabet" or "Morse code"—but for every message, there is a most efficient way to encode it, where "efficient" means using the fewest possible letters or symbols (or bits, or units of information). What "fewest" boils down to depends on the *information content* of the message. Shannon invented a way of measuring the information content of a message and called it *information entropy*.

Data compression is a practical application of Shannon's research, which asks, "How compact can we make a message before we can no longer recover it?"[2]

---

[2] It's important to note that according to modern information theory, there is a point at which removing any more bits removes the ability for you to uniquely recover your data stream properly. So, our compression goal is to remove as many bits as possible to get to this point, and then remove no more.

So wait...why is he infuriating?

Well, although we can thank Mr. Shannon for helping to create the modern computers on which this book is being typed (and on which you're most likely reading it), his work on information theory is directly the thing we're trying to defeat. You can look at data compression as a rebellion against information entropy. Every compression algorithm computer scientists write tries to disprove Claude Shannon's research, and *compress the data further than its measured entropy.* We scrape and pull and steal any bits we can from a message, to make it as small as possible, each time trying to break below Shannon's definition of entropy and get to a new level of information understanding. Millions upon millions of hours of engineering time over the past 60 years have been solely dedicated to creating algorithms to defeat—or cleverly sneak around —a concept created by this brilliant man.

The Only Thing You Need to Know about Data Compression

OK, here's what you need.

Data compression works via two simple ideas:

- Reduce the number of unique symbols in your data (smallest possible "alphabet").
- Encode more frequent symbols with fewer bits (fewest bits for most common "letters").

Boom. Done. That's it.

Sixty years of compression research boiled down to two bullet points. Every single algorithm in data compression focuses on doing one of these two things. It transforms the data to be more compressible by shuffling or reducing the number of symbols, or it takes advantage of the fact that some symbols are more common than others, and encodes more common symbols with fewer bits.

What makes applied data compression so complex is that there's a gazillion ways to do these two things, depending on the kind of data you have. You'll need to take the following considerations into account:

- Different data needs to be treated differently. Words in a book and floating-point numbers, for example, respond to very different algorithms.
- Some data can be transformed first to make it more compressible.

- Data might be skewed. For example, temperature data taken in summer might be skewed toward high temperatures; that is, it might contain a lot more high temperatures than near-freezing ones.

Your challenge as a programmer is to figure out the best way, or combination of ways, for compressing any block of data that a user throws at your application. And your challenge as a content developer is to figure out how to throw data at your users and not break their bank accounts.[3]

That, my dear adventurer, is what the rest of this book is about. It's your field guide to understanding what in the compression world is worthy of your attention, and how the algorithms work *conceptually*, so that you can choose the right ones and apply them to your super awesome social/mobile/web/media application data.

A World Built on Data Compression

Let's be clear about this: the computing world that you live in, right now, is built entirely on the back of data compression algorithms.

Yup. Every piece of it.

Every web page, image, song, cat video, streaming Internet movie, selfie, video game download, microtransaction, and OS update works only because of compression algorithms. In fact, you can't throw a single bit of data around the Internet without running into some compressed content.

What's so amazing about data compression technology is that it's responsible for some of the largest changes in personal computing over the past 40 years, and no one knows about it.

For example, do you download or stream music instead of buying a CD? If so, you have compression to thank.

Music compression

See, in 1996, a joint working group (a bunch of smart people from different companies) unveiled the MP3 file format. This new audio format changed the nature of audio on computers. Until that point, the WAV file format was the most dominant and accepted format for creating, storing, and transferring audio data. Everyone used it, but the files were irresponsibly huge. A three-minute song could be roughly 30 MB in size and take around 9 minutes to download.[4] Forget about streaming!

---

3 Because data plans are metered and horribly expensive in most parts of the world.

4 Check out "The Web Back in 1996–1997" (*http://royal.pingdom.com/2008/09/16/the-web-in-1996-1997/*) for a historical detour.

The invention of MP3 meant that anyone could get a full-length, three-minute song as about 1–3 MB of data at impressive audio quality levels.[5] Users could even plop CDs into their computers and convert an entire album to the MP3 format to listen to digitally.

This combination of smaller file size and good quality gave birth to one of the biggest consumer innovations of our time: Napster (*https://en.wikipedia.org/wiki/Napster*). This service made it possible for people to trade MP3s with one another, free of cost. Of course, this opened up a massive legal problem: folks would buy a CD, convert the audio to MP3, and then share it with their friends, who never had to pay for the original disc. As you can imagine, the companies who make money off CD sales were infuriated and did everything within their power to successfully shut down the Napster service.

And so, the late 1990s/early 2000s were riddled with legal battles and governmental policy changes attempting to stop this kind of music sharing. There was even legislation proposed that would make the use of the MP3 format illegal.

Apple, rather than fighting this new digital phenomenon, decided to build a product around it. In 1998, it launched the iPod, one of the first portable devices dedicated to storing and playing MP3 files. With it came the iTunes Store, where customers could legally purchase MP3 files for personal use.[6]

Today digital music distribution has become the new normal, with a plethora of companies trying to find better ways to sell music to you.

The massive success of the iPod product eventually led to the development and release of the iPhone device, changing the face of personal computing forever. (But that's a different story.)

Image compression

Let's cycle back in time a bit further to the birth of the Internet. In 1978, when the first connections of the Internet structure were created, the amount of data sent was pretty minimal. The small number of users would primarily send and receive text data, or images that were created entirely out of characters, as demonstrated in Figure 1-1.[7]

---

5 Note that MP3 is a lossy data compression format; that is, some information is lost during compression. We briefly talk about this type of data compression later in the book.

6 The first portable MP3 player was launched in 1997 by SaeHan Information Systems, and AT&T set up the first streaming service.

7 ASCII art (*https://en.wikipedia.org/wiki/ASCII_art*) was actually invented by creative folks with typewriters.

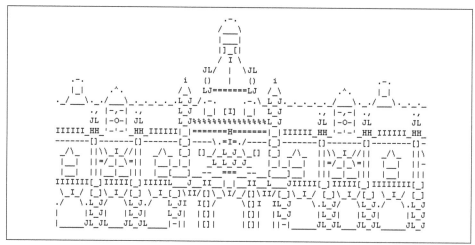

Figure 1-1. A castle, made of ASCII art. Source: Wikipedia (https://en.wikipedia.org/w/index.php?title=ASCII_art&oldid=87086275), no author.

The issue at hand was that real image information, stored in 24-bits-per-pixel format, was entirely too hefty for early connection modems. So, of course, the compression gurus went right at it. To test their new image compression algorithms, they needed a corpus of images. Being part of a male-dominated industry, they might have had a bias toward gentlemen's magazines for source material; thus, they ended up with the now famous Lena image (see Figure 1-2), a picture of Lena Söderberg (*https://en.wiki pedia.org/wiki/Lena_S%C3%B6derberg*) from the pages of the November 1972 issue of Playboy magazine.

Figure 1-2. "Lena." Original full portrait photographed by Dwight Hooker and published as "Playmate of the Month" in the November 1972 issue of Playboy magazine. This 512 x 512 electronic/mechanical scan of a section of the full portrait was created by Alexander Sawchuk et al. and is available from the USC-SIPI image database (http://bit.ly/ 28Ji2TN). Licenses under Fair Use via Wikipedia (https://en.wikipedia.org/wiki/ File:Lenna.png).

When they unveiled the results of their research, they used a cropped, PG-13 version of the image in their paper, and provided the original version for others to test their own compression algorithms on, as well. For a long time, Lena was the gold-standard corpus image for testing the majority of image compression algorithms. Thankfully, since then, less controversial image corpora have been created. (The Kodak (*http:// r0k.us/graphics/kodak/*) company's image test suite (*http://r0k.us/graphics/kodak/*) is our personal favorite.) However, Lena is often still included as a litmus test in many image compression papers today.

Video compression

Fast-forward to 2001 and the launch of YouTube, a website where users could upload any video they recorded, for free, for everyone to see.

Until this point, the dominant way of sending around video information had been in the MOV format, which was nothing more advanced than a series of JPG images strung together in order. Unsurprisingly, the files were insanely large. So, the idea that you could just load a web page and watch a video was mind-boggling.

Genome mapping

In 2008, in an attempt to tackle disease and human mortality, scientists started to map and test the human genome. A single genome sequence represents an enormous amount of data—more than 14 GB just to describe the makeup of a human. These data sizes were larger than most systems were able to handle (and cloud computing hadn't become a big thing yet).

Compression, once again, came to the rescue. Researchers were able to find that BWT[8] was the most efficient way to store DNA information in a compressed form, and they could even perform operations on it without having to decompress it first.

By 2014, researchers had created one of the fastest protein folders on the planet, combining scalable cloud computing and compressed data transfer between host computers.

Compression and the economy

So, you see, compression has been at the heart of many massive changes in computing technology and culture. The reason for this lies in simple economic theory: compressed files are smaller files. Meaning, it takes less time to transfer them, and it costs less to do so, as well. Distributors pay less to distribute, and customers pay less to consume. In a modern world in which computing time is literally money, compression represents the most economically viable way to shorten the gap between content distributors and content consumers.

---

8 We'll explore Burrows–Wheeler transform (*https://en.wikipedia.org/wiki/Burrows%E2%80%93Wheeler_trans form*) deeply in Chapter 8.

CHAPTER 2

Do Not Skip This Chapter

Even if you are familiar with *binary numbers*, DO NOT SKIP THIS CHAPTER. We are going to begin digging into *information theory* as well, which is required for understanding the rest of this book.

Understanding Binary

It might seem a bit odd to start a book about data compression with a primer on binary numbers. Bear with us here. Everything in data compression is about reducing the number of bits used to represent a given data set. To expand on this concept, and the ramifications of its mathematics, let's just take a second and make sure everyone is on the same page.

Base 10 System

Modern human mathematics is built around the decimal—base 10—number system.[1]

This system makes it possible for us to use the digits [0,1,2,3,4,5,6,7,8,9] strung together to represent number values. Back in elementary school, you might have been exposed to the concept of numeric columns, where, for example, the value 193 is split into three columns of hundreds, tens, and ones.

Hundreds	Tens	Ones
1	9	3

---

[1] For now. We are sure quantum computing or Babylonian counting will change this one day.

Effectively, 193 is equivalent to 1 * 100 + 9 * 10 + 3. And as soon as you grasped that pattern, maybe you realized that you could count to any number.

Later, when you learned about exponents, you were able to replace the "hundreds" and "tens" with their "base ten to the power" equivalents, and a new pattern emerged.

10^2	10^1	10^0
1	9	3

So:

$$193 = 1 * 100 + 9 * 10 + 3 = (1 * 10^2) + (9 * 10^1) + (3 * 10^0)$$

Because each column can contain only a single-digit number, what happens when we add another 1 to 9? Counting up from 9 gives us 10 (two digits). So, we keep the zero in our current 10^0 column and shift the 1 to the next column to the left, which is 10^1 and happens to represent "tens."

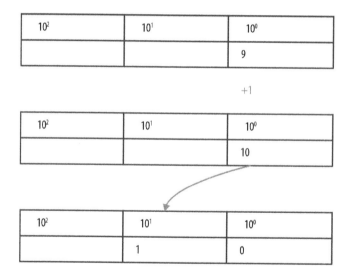

10^2	10^1	10^0
		9

+1

10^2	10^1	10^0
		10

10^2	10^1	10^0
	1	0

As we count up further, we hit 19 + 1 = two tens (2 * 10^1), and by the time we get to 99, yep, we shift left for 1 * 10^2.

Binary Number System

The binary number system works under the exact same principles as the decimal system, except that it operates in base 2 rather than base 10. So, instead of columns in the table being powers to the base of ten:

$10^2 \mid 10^1 \mid 10^0$

they are powers to a base of two:

$2^2 \mid 2^1 \mid 2^0$

Instead of having available the digits 0–9 before we have to shift, we can only use 0–1.

Counting in binary becomes "zero," "one," and because 2^1 is the next column already, "two" is 1-0, "three" becomes 1-1, and "four," being 2^2, shifts us over again to 1-0-0.

2^2	2^1	2^0
		1

$+1$

2^2	2^1	2^0
		10

2^2	2^1	2^0
	1	0

Converting from binary to decimal

As you were reading the previous section, we'll bet that your brain already converted the small binary numbers into their decimal equivalents, because unless you work with binary numbers all the time, you understand the value of a binary number by its decimal equivalent.

Let's be explicit and say we have the binary number 1010 and fill it into our powers columns.

2^3	2^2	2^1	2^0
1	0	1	0

To get the equivalent decimal number, we add up the values of the columns that have a 1 in them. The preceding table yields the following:

$$2^3 + 2^1 = 8 + 2 = 10$$

Thus, binary 1010 equals decimal 10.

Conversion from binary to decimal is straightforward. Converting from decimal to binary is a little more complicated.

Converting from decimal to binary

An easy method for converting a decimal number to its binary equivalent is to repeatedly divide it by two and string together the remainders, which are either "1" or a "0."

This is easiest understood by doing. So, let's convert the decimal number 294 into its binary-number equivalent using that method.

1. We begin by dividing 294 by 2, which gives us 147 with a remainder of 0.
2. We divide the result 147 by 2, which is 73 plus a reminder of 1.
3. Dividing 73 by 2, we continue to build up the table that follows.

Note that if the decimal number being divided is even, the result will be whole and the remainder will be equal to 0. If the decimal number is odd, the result will not divide completely, and the remainder will be a 1.

Number as it's divided by 2			
294	Column equivalent		
147	remainder	0 (LSB)	2^0
73	remainder	1	2^1
36	remainder	1	2^2
18	remainder	0	2^3
9	remainder	0	2^4
4	remainder	1	2^5
2	remainder	0	2^6
1	remainder	0	2^7
0	remainder	1 (MSB)	2^8

Now arrange all the remainders from right to left, with the *least significant bit (LSB)* on the right, and the *most significant bit (MSB)* on the left:

100100110

There you have it: 100100110 is the binary equivalent of decimal 294, obtained using the divide-by-2 decimal-to-binary conversion technique.

When It Works, It Works

It turns out that this divide-by-the-base method also works for conversion to other number bases. One base used commonly in computer science is base 16, or hexadecimal. Because we don't have a digit to represent decimal 11, we use the letter A for 10, B for 11, until F for 15. Try converting the number 3053 to hexadecimal by dividing by 16, and lining up the reminders from right to left. Hint: the result is pretty sleepy.

Information Theory

Now that we're all on the same page with the binary system, let's talk about what this means in the context of *information theory (https://en.wikipedia.org/wiki/Informa tion_theory)*.

in·for·ma·tion the·o·ry
> (*noun*)

>> the mathematical study of the coding of information in the form of sequences of symbols, impulses, etc., and of how rapidly such information can be transmitted, e.g., through computer circuits or telecommunications channels.

According to information theory, the information content of a number is equal to the number of binary (yes/no) decisions that you need to make before you can uniquely identify that number in a set.

Every Child Is an Expert in Applied Information Theory

The game *20 Questions (https://en.wikipedia.org/wiki/Twenty_Questions)* is a perfect illustration of the information content concept. The way we played it was that the first player would think up whatever they wanted, and the other player(s) had to figure out what it might be by asking at most 20 questions that could be answered by "yes" or "no."

Being kids, we varied the game by restricting the domain (it has to be an animal), or letting the game only go until you had gotten "no" as an answer 10 times (and, without shame, the first player resorted to lying or changing the object if someone was too quick at figuring out the answer).

The game suggests that the information required to identify an arbitrary object is at most 20 bits. Mathematically, if each question is structured to eliminate half the objects, 20 questions will actually allow the questioner to distinguish between 2^{20} or 1,048,576 objects.

That's an awful lot of objects.

We can take this one step further.

Consider this narrative setting: There is a 10 × 10–foot tiled state room with a vaulted ceiling. It has a four-poster king-sized bed facing the eastern window, a small, antique writing table along the north wall, and a heavy 18th-century armoire to the west of the bed.

You could write all of this up in a page of *JSON* or your favorite scripting language.

Or you could do it a bit differently: encode the 100 tiles of the grid using 7 bits, the four cardinal directions with 2 bits, and the three pieces of furniture with 2 bits each. Arranged in an order of tile-furniture-direction, your bed might be described as 10010100111. (The meta-information on the "meaning" of the bit codes can be in your head, coded into the software assembling the room, or attached to the data).

Now, the entire room takes 44 bits to describe—or 6 bytes—which is quite some savings from the full text or a JSON file, if you ask us. (Or just ask the mobile users who are downloading your game.)

This is a process of data compression in a nutshell.

An Excursion into Binary Search

Suppose that we're given a sorted range of numbers in an array, say 0–15, and we'd like to find where the number 10 exists in the array.

The *binary search* algorithm works by dividing the data set in the array in half, and determining if 10 is greater or smaller than the pivot value at the center.[2] Depending on the result of this decision, we split the array and keep the part of the data set that contains 10. We then compare to the new pivot value and split again. We keep splitting until all we have left is the number 10. (If this sounds a little bit like playing *20 Questions*, that's because it is!)

Now, while searching for the number, each time we decide on greater or smaller, let's output a single bit to a stream, to represent which decision we've made (0 for smaller, 1 for greater).

This is much easier to understand when you do it, so let's play this out in a fancy diagram, which you can see in Figure 2-1.

---

2 If the array has an even number of elements, there is not really a center. We just choose whether to go with the left-of-center or right-of-center element. It doesn't matter which.

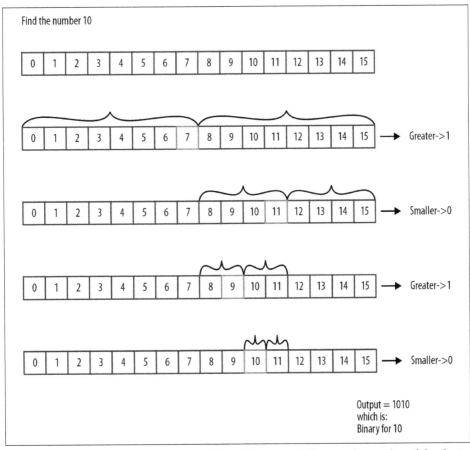

Figure 2-1. Binary search on a restricted number space. When we keep a log of the decisions (high/low) at each level, we end up with the binary version of the number.

The resulting output stream is the binary value 1010, which interestingly enough, is exactly the binary representation for the number 10. We were able to represent the number by logging how many yes/no decisions we needed to uniquely describe it, in the given set of data with length $2^n - 1$.

If you want to be left alone at a party, start talking to people about this topic. It's a sure-fire way to become the awkward person standing near the chips and dip.

Entropy: The Minimum Bits Needed to Represent a Number

So, given a random integer value, we can convert that value to binary form. Sadly, though, if given a number, it's not instantly obvious how many bits it will require without going through the process of binary conversion. This is a boring process, but thankfully, mathematics has produced a formula that makes it easier for us:[3]

$\log_2(x) = -(\log(x) / \log(2))$ = number of binary digits needed to represent a number

Mathematically speaking, $\log_2$ will return a floating-point number.

For example, $\log_2(10) = 3.321$ bits.

Technically speaking, you can't represent 3.321 bits on modern computer hardware (because we can't represent fractions of bits), so we are forced to round up to the next whole integer, using the ceil (or ceiling) function (*https://en.wikipedia.org/wiki/Floor_and_ceiling_functions*), updating our formula like so (this is a spiffed-up version, so we are going to use spiffed-up capital letters to make the distinction):

$LOG2(x) = ceil(\log(x) / \log(2))$

Of course, now there is another problem: technically, we're off by one bit for powers of two.

Take the number 2 (or any power of 2 for that matter):

$LOG2(2) = ceil(\log(2) / \log(2)) = 1$

$LOG2(4) = ceil(\log(4) / \log(2)) = 2$

The result is true from a mathematics perspective, but fails in the fact that we need two and three bits to represent the numbers 2 (bin = 10) and 4 (bin = 100) on our system. As such, we add a slight skewing to our method to ensure that our log results are accurate for powers of two.

$LOG2(x) = ceil(\log(x+1) / \log(2))$

---

3 Sorry about the math, but this one is foundational for all that follows.

Just to help you understand this concept a bit more, here's a table that displays some interesting data about LOG2 and the number of bits required to represent numbers:

Value	LOG2(value)	Binary value
0	1	0
1	1	1
2	2	10
3	2	11
4	3	100
7	3	111
15	4	1111
255	8	11111111
65535	16	1111111111111111
9.332622e+157	525	....

So, given any decimal integer number, we can easily determine the minimum number of bits needed to represent it in binary by calculating its LOG2. Shannon defined this LOG2 of a variable as its *entropy*, or rather, the least number of bits required to represent that value.

Standard Number Lengths

The LOG2 form of numbers is efficient but not practical for the way we build computer components.

The issue lies between representing the number in the least bits possible, confusion on how to decode a binary string of numbers (without knowing their LOG2 lengths), and performance in hardware execution.

Modern computers compromise by using fixed-length buckets of bits for numbers of different sizes. The fundamental bucket is one byte, which is made up of eight bits. And the integer buckets typically available in modern programming languages are a short with 16 bits, an integer with 32 bits, and a long with 64 bits. As such, our decimal number 10, converted to binary as 1010, would be a short and represented as 0000000000001010. This is a lot of wasted bits.

The point here is that the majority of algorithms we use in the development of modern applications all tend to use defined bit ranges rather than the LOG2 size. Which is basically the difference between information theory and implementation practicality. Any bit stream we have will always be rounded up to the next byte-aligned size in computer memory. This can get confusing: for example, when we've just saved 7 bits of data, our machine reports that our data still remains the same number of bytes long.

The goal in practical data compression is to get as close as possible to the theoretical limit of compressibility. That's why, to learn and understand compression algorithms, moving forward with the rest of this book, we will only think in terms of LOG2.

CHAPTER 3

Breaking Entropy

Understanding Entropy

Because he had nothing better to do, Dr. Shannon called the LOG2 version of a number *entropy*, or the smallest number of bits required to represent a value. He further extended the concept of entropy (why not recycle terminology...) to entire data sets, where you could describe the smallest number of bits needed to represent the entire data set. He worked out all the math and gave us this lovely formula for H(s)[1] as the Entropy of a Set:

$$H(s) = -\sum_{i=1}^{n} p_i log_2(p_i)$$

This might look rather intimidating,[2] so let's pick it apart:[3]

---

[1] Shannon denoted entropy with the term H (capital Greek letter Eta), named after Boltzmann's H-theorem (*https://en.wikipedia.org/wiki/H-theorem*).

[2] Note, the formula for H uses the mathematical definition of $log_2()$, which is different from the LOG2() we defined in Chapter 2. In this case, we don't expect the output to be rounded up to the next highest integer, and the value is allowed to be negative.

[3] You can find implementations of this algorithm in various languages over at Rosetta Code (*http://rosetta code.org/wiki/Entropy*).

en·tro·py
  (noun)

  A thermodynamic quantity representing the unavailability of a system's thermal energy for conversion into mechanical work, often interpreted as the degree of disorder or randomness in the system. (wrt physics)

  Lack of order or predictability; gradual decline into disorder. (wrt H.P. Lovecraft)

  A logarithmic measure of the rate of transfer of information in a particular message or language. (in information theory)

To be practical and concrete, let's begin with a group of letters; for example:

G = [A,B,B,C,C,C,D,D,D,D][4]

First, we calculate the set *S* of the data grouping *G*. (This is "set" in the mathematical sense: a group of numbers that occur only once, and whose ordering doesn't matter.)

S = set(G) = [A,B,C,D]

This is the set of unique symbols in G.

Next, we calculate the probability of occurrence for each symbol in the set.

Here is the mathematical formula:

$$P(v_i) = count(v_i)/len(G)$$

What this means is that the frequency or probability *P* of a symbol *v* is the number of times that symbol occurs in set *G* (that is, count(*v*)), divided by the length of the set *G*.

Shifting from math to tables, let's figure out the probability of each symbol inside of *G*. Because we have 10 symbols in *G*, *len*(*G*) is 10, and thus the probability for each symbols is a multiple of 0.1:

---

4 It doesn't matter whether the values are sorted; that is, it has no effect on entropy, as we'll see later in the chapter. We chose this ordering because it's easy to see how many there are of each letter.

Symbol	Count	Probability
A	1	0.1
B	2	0.2
C	3	0.3
D	4	0.4
	Total must be:	1.0

With the probabilities for our unique symbols calculated, we can now go ahead and compute the Shannon entropy H of the set G. Gaze again upon this lovely formula; and fear not, as the gist is much simpler than you might think:

$$H(s) = -\sum_{i=1}^{n} p_i log_2(p_i)$$

Firstly, for each symbol, multiply the probability of that symbol against log_2 of the probability of that symbol. Secondly, add it all up, and voilà, you've got your entropy for the set.

So, let's apply this to G.

Symbol Σ	Probability p	$log_2(p)$	$p * log_2(p)$
1	0.1	-3.321	-0.3321
2	0.2	-2.321	-0.4642
3	0.3	-1.736	-0.5208
4	0.4	-1.321	-0.5284
		SUM	-1.8455

Summing that last column together gives a value of -1.8455 (give or take a few *qubits*). The Entropy equation applies a final sign inversion (that minus sign before the big Σ), giving us ~1.8455 bits per symbol to represent this dataset… Ta-da!

What This Entropy Stuff Is Good For

Because G = [A,B,B,C,C,C,D,D,D,D] has an entropy of $H(G)$ = ~1.8455, we can roughly say that G can be encoded by using 2 bits per value (by rounding up to the next whole bit).

We assign the following 2-bit character encodings:

A -> 00

B -> 01

C -> 10

D -> 11

Our binary-encoded grouping G^e then looks like this:

e = [00,01,01,10,10,10,11,11,11,11]

With this encoding, we end up with a size of G^e (denoted as $|G^e|$ in most texts) as 20 bits.

Now for the fun part: We can calculate the final size of G^e without having to actually do the encoding step. All we have to do is multiply the rounded-up[5] entropy value H by the length of G ($|G|$):

$H(G) * |G| = 2 * 10 = 20$ bits $= |G^e|$

And according to Shannon entropy, that's as small as you can make this data set.[6]

So, wrapping all this up, entropy generally represents the minimum number of bits per symbol, on average, that you need in order to encode your data set so as to produce the smallest version of it.

Understanding Probability

At its core, Shannon entropy is built upon the evaluation of the probability of symbols in the data stream, in an inverse sort of way.

Basically, the more frequently a symbol occurs, the less it contributes to the overall information content of the data set. Which…seems completely counter-intuitive.

We can find a real-world example of this in fishing. Suppose that you are sitting at the shoreline, reel and rod and fancy hat, in your lawn chair, watching the river and your bobber. Every few minutes, you take note of the state of the bobber, which remains unchanged. But every hour or so, a fish bites. That's the thing you are interested in! So, very low information over a long time, with the occasional really important thing happening. If you represented the measurements you take with 0 for "no fish" and 1 for "fish!", you could easily write your notes as 00000000010000000001000000000001.

---

5 Remember that in practice we can't represent fractional bits...yet.

6 Which is a complete and utter lie...but we'll get to that in a minute.

Statistically (and sportingly!) speaking, the interesting parts are the events when the fish are biting. The rest is just redundancy.

But enough metaphor, let's take a look at a few numerical examples. The next table shows some sets of probabilities (we don't care about the actual symbols for now) and their associated entropies:

Probability set $P(G)$	Entropy $H(G)$	For a set of 1000 symbols...
[0.001, 0.002, 0.003, 0.994]	0.06	994 would be the same
[0.25, 0.25, 0.003, 0.497]	1.53	497 would be the same
[0.1, 0.1, 0.4, 0.4]	1.72	800 would be equally shared by two symbols
[0.1, 0.2, 0.3, 0.4]	1.84	One symbol would dominate but not by much
[0.25, 0.25, 0.25, 0.25]	2	Each symbol would occur 250 times

So, what's going on here?

In the first row, the fourth symbol claims the overwhelming majority of the probability. This data set is dominantly composed of that one symbol, with a sprinkling of the others somewhere in it randomly. Because one symbol contributes to so much of the data stream's content, it means there's less overall information in the data set, hence the lower entropy value.

In the last row of the table, you can see that all four symbols are equally probable, and thus they contribute equally to the data stream's content. The result is that there's more information in the data set, and therefore we need more bits, per symbol, to represent it.

For example, playing whack-a-mole is interesting because all slots are equally probable, and you never know from which one the mole is going to pop up, which is what makes it a lot more interesting than fishing.

Breaking Entropy

The bleeding edge of data compression is all about messing with this entropy. In fact, the entire science of compression is about calling entropy a big fat liar on the Internet.

The truth is that, in practice,[7] it's entirely possible to compress data to a form smaller than defined by entropy. We do this by exploiting two properties of real data. Entropy, as defined by Shannon, cares only about probability of occurrence, regard-

---

7 Take that, "Theory"!

less of symbol ordering. But ordering is one fundamental piece of information for real data sets, and so are relationships between symbols.

For example, these two sets, the ordered [1,2,3,4] and the unordered [4,1,2,3], have the same entropy, but you intuitively recognize that there is additional information in that ordering. Or using letters, [Q,U,A,R,K] and [K,R,U,Q,A] also have the same entropy. But not only does [Q,U,A,R,K] represent a word with meaning in the English language, there are rules about the occurrence of letters. For example, Q is usually followed by U.

Let's look at some examples of how we can exploit these properties to break entropy. (Roll up your sleeves, we're gonna compress some data!)

The key to breaking entropy is to exploit the structural organization of a data set to transform its data into a new representation that has a lower entropy than the source information.

Example 1: Delta Coding

Let's take a set of increasing numbers, [0,1,2,3,4,5,6,7], and call it set A.

Now, shuffle that set to get set B = [1,0,2,4,3,5,7,6].

These two sets have a few unique characteristics with respect to information theory:

- All the symbols are equally probable, and there are no duplicates.
- Set A and set B have the same exact entropy of H = 3.

So, according to Dr. Shannon, we should assign 3 bits per symbol, requiring 24 bits total to encode each set. It turns out that it is possible to easily break entropy and encode set A in fewer bits. Here is how:

Set A is effectively just a linearly increasing run of numbers. So, instead of encoding each number, we could transform the stream and encode each number by its difference from the previous one. Set A encoded would then look like this:

[0,1,1,1,1,1,1,1]

And the entropy of this stream is only H(A) = 1. Not bad, eh?

This type of transform is known as *Delta Coding*, or the process of encoding a series of numbers as the difference from the previous number.[8]

---

8 Don't worry, we'll talk about this in more depth in Chapter 8.

So let's talk about set B. Because it's not linearly increasing, delta coding won't really work on it, as we'd get [1,–1,2,2,–1,2,2,–1] with an entropy of H(B) = 2, which doesn't look so bad at first. However, first we would need to encode the *multiset*[9] B as [01,00,10,10,00,10,10,00] using a total of 16 bits. In addition, we'd also need to store for the decoder that the codeword "00" represents the symbol –1, which takes up additional space. So, not much of a win, if any. (In fact, for some sets, delta coding might even require more bits overall than just encoding the data directly.)

Ordering Matters!

Entropy says that the ordering of symbols doesn't matter, but delta coding proves that to not be the case. If there's a high correlation between two adjacent values, delta coding can transform the data in such a way that it changes the entropy to a lower value.

Example 2: Symbol Grouping

Suppose that you have a string S = "TOBEORNOTTOBEORTOBEORNOT", which has the unique set of symbols [O,T,B,E,R,N] and entropy $H(S) = 2.38$.

Any human can look at this and realize that there are duplicate words here. So, what if instead of using individual letters as symbols, we used words? This gives us the unique set [TO,BE,OR,NOT] and an entropy of $H(S) = 1.98$.

So, if using words instead of symbols has given us a lower entropy value for the stream, how far can we take this? It looks like the term "TOBEORNOT" is used multiple times. Could we collapse that into one symbol?

Let's just try that:

set(S)=[TOBEORNOT,TO,BE,OR] with an entropy $H(S)=1.92$[10]

Take that, entropy![11]

---

9 A multiset is a set for which multiple occurrences of the same element are allowed.

10 Of course, although in theory there is a difference between the two ways of grouping, for this tiny data set, in practice, we'd still need 2 bits either way. But remember that right now we are only concerned with beating Shannon.

11 It's worth pointing out that there's a sweet spot with respect to symbol grouping, and an entire field of data transforms that help you find the optimal parsing; they are called "Dictionary Encoders," and we will discuss them in Chapter 7.

Example 3: Permutations

The interesting thing about set B [1,0,2,4,3,5,7,6] from Example 1 is that it's a shuffled version, or permutation, of set A [0,1,2,3,4,5,6,7].

> In mathematics, the notion of permutation relates to the act of rearranging, or permuting, all the members of a set into some sequence or order.

Effectively, a permutation is a shuffled version of an original set for which the order of elements matters, and no items are repeated. From a classical definition, permutations only exist as a shuffling of a run of numbers. For example [2,1,3,4] is a valid permutation of [1,2,3,4], whereas [5,2,7,9] is not.

Permutations are notoriously difficult to compress. (Some would say impossibly difficult, but we are not sure they really understand the meaning of that word). The reason for this is simple: according to entropy, a permutation is incompressible, because there's no information in the ordering itself (because it's not ordered anymore). Each value is equally probable, and thus takes the same number of bits to represent.

The size of the encoded set Q = [2,1,3,0] is $len(Q) * \log_2(max(Q)) = 8$ bits,[12] which we can generalize to N * LOG2(N). Keep this number in mind. As you begin to explore more of compression, information theory, and entropy, this value will continue to kick you square in the face as a glaring reminder of how little you matter in the universe.

---

12 The maximum value of a set A of elements is denoted by max(A) and is equal to the last element of a sorted (i.e., ordered) version of A.

Compressing Permutations by Using Elimination Coding

So, remember how we said permutations weren't compressible? We lied to you. It wasn't a big lie, but it was a necessary lie to let you understand the gravity of the situation. We are sorry for that. In truth, permutations are slightly compressible, but not enough to be really interesting or of any practical use. Let us show you how.

Let's begin with set C = [5, 7, 1, 4, 6, 3, 2, 0].

Encoding this by the number values in the set, with 3 bits, dictated by the maximum value 7, yields:

101 111 001 100 110 011 010 000

which is 24 bits long.

Now, let's encode "by the index," instead. It works like this. (You might want to follow along using old-fashioned paper and pencil.)

Round 1

Create an array with eight empty, indexed slots to hold the numbers.

0	1	2	3	4	5	6	7	Number
0	1	2	3	4	5	6	7	Index

1. Start with the first number in the set, which is 5.

2. Calculate its Free-Slot-Index: find the index of the slot with the value of our number. In our case, 5 is at index 5.

3. Determine how many bits you need to encode the Free-Slot-Index. This is done by calculating LOG2 of the number of slots. Because there are 8 slots, LOG2(8) = 3 bits. So, we encode the number 5 using 3 bits, which is 101.

4. Now, remove the slot with value 5 from the array.

The output stream contains: 101

The new working array is:

0	1	2	3	4	6	7
0	1	2	3	4	5	6

Round 2

1. Take the next number in the set C = [5, 7, 1, 4, 6, 3, 2, 0], which is 7.

2. Free-Slot-Index: find the index of the slot with the value of your number. This time, 7 is at index 6.

3. There are 7 free slots left, and LOG2(7) = 3. So, we output Free-Slot-Index 6 using 3 bits as 110.

4. Remove the slot with value 7 from the array.

Output stream: 101 110

New working array:

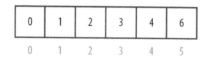

Round 3

1. Take the next number in C, which is 1.

2. Free-Slot-Index: find the index of the slot with the value of your number. In our case, it's at index 1.

3. Calculate the LOG2 of the total number of free slots, where LOG2(6) = 3. Output the index 1 using 3 bits as 001.

4. Remove the slot with value 1.

Output stream: 101 110 001

New working array:

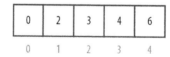

Round 4

1. The next number in the set is 4.

2. Its Free-Slot-Index is 3.

3. There remain 5 free slots, so LOG2(5) = 3 bits.

4. Output index 3 using the 3 bits as 011.

5. Remove the slot with value 4.

Output stream: 101 110 001 011

Round 5

Now things are finally starting to get interesting.

(We are halfway through our set [~~5, 7, 1, 4~~, 6, 3, 2, 0]).

1. Our next number is 6.
2. Its Free-Slot-Index is 3.
3. At this point, the number of free slots has dropped to 4, so LOG2(4) = 2, and we now only need 2 bits to encode an index.
4. Output 3 using 2 bits as 11.
5. Remove the slot with value 6.

Output stream: 101 110 001 011 11

Finishing up

1. The next number is 3.
2. It's at Free-Slot-Index 2.
3. We encode with 2 bits as 10.
4. Remove the slot with value 3.

Output stream: 101 110 001 011 11 10

0 | 2
0 | 1

1. The next number 2, at Free-Slot-Index 1, can be encoded with 1 bit.
2. And we encode 0 with the last Free-Slot-Index, 0, using also 1 bit.

Final Output stream: 101 110 001 011 11 10 1 0

Length: 18 bits

And here is how this works out saving 6 bits. Look at the table to compare:

Output:

Input	5	7	1	4	6	3	2	0
Index	5	6	1	3	3	2	1	0
Bits	101	110	001	011	11	10	1	0

Instead of encoding the numbers, which would cost us 24 bits, by encoding the indexes, we only need 18 bits—a savings of about 25%. So, we've seen how this saves us bits, but...

Why does this save us bits?

Statistics says that for a permutation, there are N! (aka factorial(N)) possible combinations (for an array of length N, where each value is between 0–N and never repeated). So, when the first value is used, we know that it can't be used again anywhere else. This means that for the second value, we have (N - 1)! options left. The third value has (N - 2)! options left (and so on). At some point, LOG((N - X)!) of the indexes will become less than LOG(N!) of the permutation by a full integer value. As such, we can identify which of the remaining options we have left, by using fewer bits.

This method works regardless of the size of the permutation. If you encode content this way, you'll always be ensured to produce a final stream smaller than entropy. For example, if you have a permutation containing all of the numbers from 0 to 65,535, you can compress it to only 90% of the original space, regardless of how shuffled it is. In practice this doesn't usually buy you enough space to make it worthwhile.

Decoding works in the opposite manner. You begin with a blank array of slots and read the next LOG2(#OpenSlots) bits from the stream, representing the number of blank spaces to count, to determine what the source number was.

1. We have 8 free slots, so we read the first 3 bits from the input stream, which are 101.

2. 101 is the binary version of 5. At index 5 we have the number 5, so our first numbers is 5. Now we remove that slot from the free slot list.

3. We have 7 free slots, reading LOG2(7) = 3 bits, giving us 110, which is decimal index 6, so the next number is 7.

4. And now it's your turn.

Information Theory Versus Data Compression

These simple experiments prove that there's some wiggle room when it comes to information theory and entropy. Remember that entropy defines the minimum number of bits required per symbol, *on average*, to encode the data stream. This means that some symbols will use fewer bits and some will use more bits than indicated by entropy.

The algorithmic *art* of data compression is really about trying to break entropy. Or rather, to transform your data in such a way that the new version has a lower entropy value. That's really the dance here: information theory sets the rules, and data compression brilliantly side-steps them with the gusto of a bullfighter.

And that's really it. That's what this entire book is about: how to apply data transformation to create lower entropy data streams (and then properly compress them). Understanding the dynamic between information theory and data compression will help you to put in perspective the give-and-take that these two have in the information world around us.

Kolmogorov Complexity

As we've already discussed, entropy is a horrible metric for evaluating compression.[13]

There exists another complexity measurement that might be more accurate, but it's not really standardized in terms of usage.

Kolmogorov complexity (*https://en.wikipedia.org/wiki/Kolmogorov_complexity*) is a measure of the computational resources needed to specify an object. It is named after Andrey Kolmogorov, who first published on the subject in 1963.

For example, consider the following two strings of 32 lowercase letters and digits:

ababababababababababababababababab

4c1j5b2p0cv4w1x8rx2y39umgw5q85s7

We could write a simple program in Python to generate the first string:

```
< v = 'ab' * 16 >
```

---

13 Well, to be fair, it's really good at estimating the compression when only considering statistical compressors (see Chapter 4), but as soon as you begin combining them with contextual compressors, it kinda gets thrown out the window.

Notice that the program to generate the string is smaller than the string itself. As an effective way of compression, you could just send the program to someone and have them regenerate the source string.

The second stream doesn't follow a pattern, and so the program needed to generate it is much larger than the source stream; so, no compression here.

Here's a handy primer:

Entropy
  Number of yes/no questions needed to uniquely describe a piece of data.

Kolmogorov complexity
  The size of the program needed to uniquely generate your data.

It can be shown that the Kolmogorov complexity of any string cannot be more than a few bytes larger than the length of the string itself (basically, a program that writes out each element of the string). Strings whose Kolmogorov complexity is small relative to the string's size, like the 'abab' example above, are not considered to be complex.

Kolmogorov complexity really begins to shine when you start talking about using *logic synthesis* (*https://en.wikipedia.org/wiki/Logic_synthesis*) or *program synthesis* (*https://en.wikipedia.org/wiki/Program_synthesis*) for compression, which in essence take the bit stream of your data set and reverse-generate a program that will uniquely generate it.

To be fair, this is all kinda hand-wavy. Entropy is far from the best solution, but it's a "good enough" metric that most folks rely on it. Discovering a more accurate solution might involve a lot of random searches through data information and analysis space. The main point here is that, despite being around for almost 50 years, data compression science is still young. We don't have all the answers, and really, that's what you should be helping with.

Variable-Length Codes

The examples in the previous chapter showed two things: we can save bits by encoding some symbols with fewer or more bits than others, and that this doesn't work well when there are duplicate symbols in the data set. And let's face it, real-life data sets are full of duplicates.

This, at its core, is why the LOG2 number system doesn't properly represent the true information content of a data set. This chapter shows how you can do some nifty things based on probability and duplication that can yield impressive compression results.

Morse Code

To begin talking about transmitting real-life data, let's go way back to the age of the telegraph and Morse code.

Beginning in 1836, American artist Samuel F. B. Morse, American physicist Joseph Henry, and American machinist Alfred Vail developed an electrical telegraph system. This system sent pulses of electric current[1] along wires, and the pulses interacted with an electromagnet that was located at the receiving end of the telegraph system, creating audible taps, or, when a paper (ticker) tape was moved under the thing doing the tapping at a constant rate, a paper record of the signals received.

The telegraph was a fantastic invention in terms of being able to communicate human information across long distances. Eventually losing the wires (see Figure 4-1), it evolved into the mobile device in your pocket.

---

1 You can listen to a sample (*https://www.youtube.com/watch?v=xsDk5_bktFo*).

Figure 4-1. British post office engineers inspect Guglielmo Marconi's wireless telegraphy equipment during a demonstration on Flat Holm island, May 13, 1897. This was the world's first demonstration of the transmission of radio signals over open sea, between Lavernock Point and Flat Holm Island, a distance of three miles. Source: Wikipedia (https://commons.wikimedia.org/wiki/File:Post_Office_Engineers.jpg).

However, the developers now needed a way to represent human concepts, such as language, in a way that the signals of electric current could carry. The device itself worked very simplistically for the operator: push the telegraph key to make a connection and send current across the wire; leave the key up, and no current is sent. Even though binary code hadn't been invented yet, back in the 1800s, this system was effectively using the same idea for communicating information.

Perhaps the simplest way to encode some text information would be to number all of the English characters—A to Z—with numeric values 0–26. You could then use the number of pulses, along with pairing, to determine what digit you were transmitting. For example, you could translate "THE HAT" into 20-8-5 8-1-20. In reality, the system would also need a way to determine the differences between words, spaces, punctuation, and eventually end-of-message, but you get the gist.

Remember, though, that these signals were transmitted by a human operator banging on a telegraph key. So, "THE HAT" would cost the same number of operator actions as "FAT CAT" and "TIP TOP." This gets gets pretty crazy when you have a post office sending 100 to 200 telegrams of 50 words each, all day long. It quickly became apparent that the number of physical actions required to send a message was becoming too high. Physical hardware (the machine) and human hardware (the operator's wrist) were wearing down faster than expected. The solution was to use statistics to reduce overall work. You see, some letters in the English language are used more frequently than others. For example, E is used 12% of the time, whereas G is used only 2% of the time. If the operator is going to be banging out more "E"s during the day, we should make those as fast and easy as possible, right?

And thus, Morse code (*http://aa9pw.com/morsecode/*) was invented.

This system applied a set of long and short pulses to each character in the English alphabet; the more frequent the character, the smaller and simpler the code. Thus, the most common letter in English, the letter "E," has the shortest code, a single dot, and "X" unsurprisingly is long-ish, and all numbers use five pulses. Figure 4-2 shows the original character set.

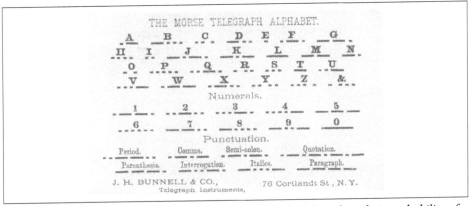

Figure 4-2. Morse code assigns dots and dashes to symbols based on their probability of occurrence in the English language. The more probable a symbol, the shorter its code. This image is an early version of Morse code, defined specifically by telegraph companies for transmitting small sets of information. Morse has evolved since then, and looks very different now.

Even back in the 1800s, this was one of the first realizations of assigning variable-length codes to symbols in order to reduce the overall amount of work that needed to be done to communicate a message.

It makes sense then that Claude Shannon (who was an expert in Morse code) would be able to take advantage of this concept in his early research of information theory to produce the first generation of a new field of technology, called "data compression," all with the help of variable-length codes.

Probability, Entropy, and Codeword Size

For the sake of data compression, our goal is simple: given symbols in a data set, assign the shortest codes to the most probable symbols.

But let's take a step back for a second and consider how entropy plays into all of this. Imagine a large data set that only contains two symbols [A,B]. We can compute the probability of each symbol ($P(A)$ and $P(B)$, respectively) and see how the probabilities affect the entropy of the set. The following table shows sample probabilities and their corresponding set entropies.

P(A)	P(B)	Entropy of set
0.99	0.01	0.08
0.9	0.1	0.47
0.8	0.2	0.72
0.7	0.3	0.88
0.6	0.4	0.97
0.5	0.5	1
0.4	0.6	0.97
0.3	0.7	0.88
0.2	0.8	0.72
0.1	0.9	0.47
0.01	0.99	0.08

A few things are immediately obvious when you look at this table:

- When $P(A) == P(B)$, both symbols are equally likely, and entropy is at its maximum value of LOG2(# symbols); thus, not very compressible.

- The more probable one symbol is, the lower the entropy value, and thus, the more compressible the data set.

- For our two-symbol set, entropy doesn't care which symbol is more probable. $H([0.9,0.1])$ is equivalent to $H([0.1,0.9])$.

This means several important things to us if we want to assign variable-length codes to a given symbol.

First, as the redundancy of the set goes down, the entropy goes up, approaching the LOG2 value of the data set.

For example, in the table that follows, we have four symbols with equal probability. The entropy of this set is $-4(0.25\log_2(0.25)) = 2$. Therefore, in this case, two is the smallest number of bits needed, on average, to represent each symbol.

Symbol	Probability	Codeword size	Codeword
A	0.25	2 bits	00
B	0.25	2 bits	01
C	0.25	2 bits	10
D	0.25	2 bits	11

Four symbols with equal probabilities and entropy of 2 require 2 bits per symbol.

Second, the more probable one symbol is, the more compressible the data set becomes because of its lower entropy.

Much like Morse code, we can improve the situation, use codewords of varying lengths, and assign the smallest codeword to the most probable symbol. So, in contrast to the previous example, consider a 4-symbol set with the skewed probabilities shown in Table 4-1.

Table 4-1. Four symbols with skewed probabilities can use variable-length codes and entropy is only 1.57

Symbol	Probability	Codeword size	Codeword[a]
A	0.49	1 bit	0
B	0.25	2 bits	10
C	0.25	3 bits	110
D	0.01	3 bits	111

[a] Wait, this looks weird, right? Why can't we assign the codewords as [0,1,00,10] for [A,B,C,D]? The magic word is "prefix property," which is basically a requirement on how to structure your codes so that you can decode them later. We're about to talk about this in a few pages, so stick with us.

Given the string AAABBCCD (as a substring of a much larger dataset), and assuming equal probabilities, we would need 16 bits, while with the skewed probabilities shown in Table 4-1, it would only require 13 bits to encode. Small savings, but important once you imagine a realistic dataset with thousands or millions of symbols.

The calculated entropy of Table 4-1 also supports its smaller compressed size. The entropy of the table is ~1.57, and thus the smallest number of bits needed, on average, to represent each symbol is 1.57 bits.

So, what do we gain by having fractional bits, given that we can't actually use fractional bits in our data stream? Keep in mind that our examples are very, very short. To obtain results close to the theoretical possibility, the input stream would need to have thousands of symbols.

Third, the length of our codewords is tied to the probability of the symbols, not the symbols themselves.

If we take our previous example and swap the probabilities of A and D, the sizes of our codewords don't change, they just get moved around, as demonstrated here:

Symbol	Probability	Codeword size
A	0.01	3
B	0.25	2
C	0.25	3
D	0.49	1

Variable-Length Codes

So, given an input data set, we can calculate the probability of the symbols involved, and then assign variable-length codes (VLCs) to the most probable symbols to achieve compression. Great!

Of course, there are two big unknowns here. First, how are we supposed to use VLCs in our applications for compression? Second, how do we build VLCs for a data set?

Using VLCs

It's basically a three-step process to encode your data using VLCs:

1. Walk through the data set and calculate the probability for all symbols.
2. Assign codewords to symbols based upon their probability; more frequent symbols are assigned smaller codewords.
3. Walk through the data set again, and when you encode a symbol, output its codeword to the compressed bit stream.

Let's dig into each stage a little more.

Calculating symbol probabilities

This process involves creating a histogram of the symbols in your data set. That is, you walk through your data and add up the occurrences of each unique symbol. The histogram depicted in Figure 4-3 is basically just a mapping between the symbol itself and its count, or frequency.

TOBEORNOTTOBEORTOBEORNOT

Symbol	Count
T	5
O	8
B	3
E	3
R	3
N	2

Figure 4-3. A sample string and its histogram, counting the number of occurrences for each character.

Assigning codewords to symbols

Next, sort your histogram by frequency of occurrence (see Figure 4-4), and assign a VLC to each symbol, beginning with the smallest codeword in the VLC set. The end result is that the more frequent the symbol, the smaller its assigned codeword, which results in data compression.

TOBEORNOTTOBEORTOBEORNOT

Symbol	Count	Code
O	8	11
T	5	00
B	3	011
E	3	101
R	3	0100
N	2	0101

Figure 4-4. After sorting our histogram by symbol count, we can assign codes to symbols. This is often called the "codeword table." Note that the codewords do not represent standard binary numbers. This is because of the importance of encoding and decoding (which we're about to discuss).

Encoding

Encoding a stream of symbols with VLCs is very straightforward. You read symbols one by one from the stream. For each symbol read, look up its variable-length code according to the codeword table and emit the bits of that codeword to the output stream. Concatenate the codes to create a single, long bit stream.

After the entire input stream has been processed, attach the symbol-to-codeword table to the head of the output stream, as illustrated in Figure 4-5, so that the decoder can use it to recover the source data.

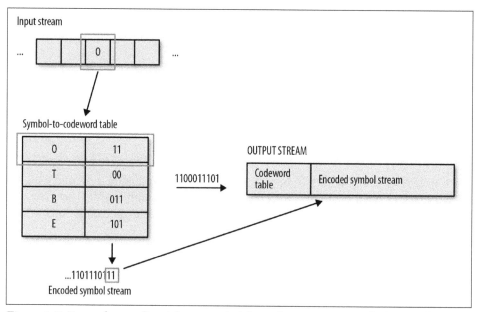

Figure 4-5. Example encoding takes a symbol from the input stream, finds its codeword, and emits the codeword to the output stream. As a final step, the symbol-to-codeword table is prepended to the output data so that the decoder can use it later.

For example, to encode the stream "TOBEORNOT" using the table we just created, the first symbol is a "T," which emits the codeword 00 to the output stream. "O" follows, outputting 11. This continues, and "TOBEORNOT" ends up as this 24-bit stream: 001101110111010001011100.

Comparing this to the 72-bit source stream (using an even 3 bits per character), we have a savings of roughly 66%.

Decoding

In general, the decoder does the inverse of the encoder. It reads some bits, checks them against the table, finds the correlated symbol, and outputs the symbol to the stream, as shown in Figure 4-6.

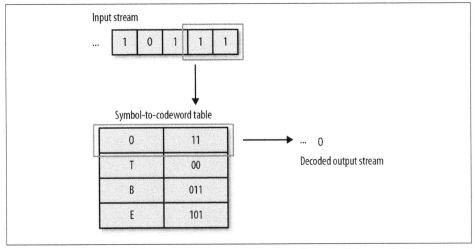

Figure 4-6. Decoding works in reverse. We read in some bits, find the symbol for those bits, and output the symbol.

However, decoding is slightly more complex because of the different lengths of the codewords. Basically, the decoder reads bits one at the time until they match one of the codewords. At that point, it outputs the associated symbol and starts reading for the next codeword.

Let's look at this with the bit stream we created, 00110111011101000101100, and use the previous table to recover our original string:

1. Read 0.
2. Check the table. There are no single-bit codewords.
3. Read 0. Find the codeword 00. Output T.
4. Read the next bit, which is 1.
5. Read 1 again. Find the codeword 11. Output O.

Now it gets more interesting:

1. Read 0, then read 1. At this point, we have multiple matches in the table. This symbol could be B, R, or N. So we read in a third bit, giving us "011." Now, we have an exact and unique match with the letter B.

2. In good tradition, decoding the rest is left as an exercise for you to carry out. After you reach the end of the bit stream, you should have recovered the original input string. (Or just refer to Figure 4-7.)

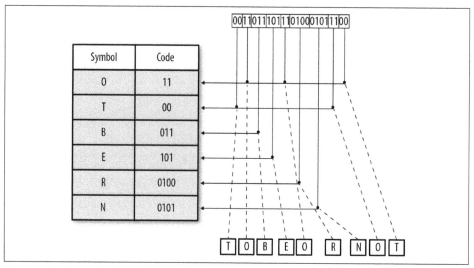

Figure 4-7. Example decoding. We read in each codeword, find the associated symbol in the codeword table, and emit it to the output stream.

Creating VLCs

We want to take a second and point out a small nuance in Morse code. Consider the following Morse encoded message:

•••

Can you figure out what the message is?

Looking back at our table, these three dots appear to be an "S" value.

Take a second look, though. This might also be three E symbols in a row (one dot each).

The ability for an operator to determine which symbol it is has to do with a bit of cheating. See, there are a lot of other things an operator can do to determine what symbol it is. For example, there's little chance that "eee" would be a valid message in the 1800s, especially if the operator knew its context (CATEEE is not a valid English word, but CATS is).

"Fist" Fights

Technically speaking, in the real world, senders can "cheat" by separating symbols with very short pauses. But pauses aren't uniform, and vary depending on the patterning of the person sending the message. The variation of individual operators in their signal durations is called their "fist," and it's unique to each person. Experienced operators, in fact, can recognize specific individuals by their fist alone, and there was even a concept of having a "good fist" or a "poor fist," which related to the clarity of the messages sent by a specific operator.

This extra work that an operator can do to determine the message is not something we can duplicate in the world of compression. We only have 0s and 1s without spaces to work with. As such, Morse code doesn't work too well as a set of codewords. Instead, we need to find a way to bind 0s and 1s together that lets the decoder uniquely decipher the resulting stream.

The prefix property

So, at any given moment, the decoder needs to be able to take a look at the bits read so far and determine whether they uniquely match the codeword for a symbol, or whether it needs to read another bit. To do this properly, the codewords of the VLC set must take into account two principles:

- Assign short codes to the most frequent symbols
- Obey the prefix property

Let's take a look at how a potential VLC can fall over. Assume the bit stream 0101111 and the following VLC table:

Symbol	Codeword
A	0
B	10
C	101
D	111

Then, the decoding process looks like this:

1. The decoder sees 0, which is unambiguously A. So it outputs A.
2. The decoder sees 1, which can be the beginning of B, C, or D.

3. The decoder reads another 0, which narrows the choice to B or C.

4. The decoder reads 1. This presents an ambiguity. In our bits read, 101, do we have 10 + 1, representing a B plus the beginning of a new symbol B, C, or D?

or

Do we have 101 for a symbol C?

At this point, you can no longer continue with the decoding process, because you've lost the ability to determine what type of value is being read in. Your choice of codewords has made it impossible to uniquely distinguish between different symbols, as illustrated in Figure 4-8.

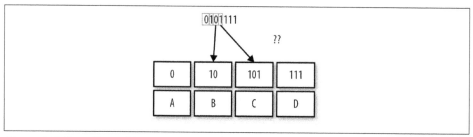

Figure 4-8. Decoding a binary stream with VLCs can be difficult if one code is the prefix of another code.

In comes the VLC *prefix property*, which dictates:

> After a code has been assigned to a symbol, no other code can start with that bit pattern.

In other words, each symbol is unambiguously identifiable by its prefix, which is the only way in which VLCs can work.

The prefix property is required for a VLC to work properly. This means that VLCs will tend to be larger compared to binary representation.

The general trade-off is that you get a larger code, but you can decode it without knowing anything about symbol size in advance. And because you have some very short codewords for common symbols, VLCs give great compression for symbol streams for which a small number of symbols have very high probability.

A Handful of Example VLCs

In this section, we are going to introduce you to a handful of VLCs that, historically, were commonly used and useful in real life. Choosing the right VLC and assigning the right codes to your symbols is another challenge altogether, as we'll briefly discuss.

How Were These VLC Codes Built?

Well, back in the day, it was all blood, sweat, and tears. A mathematician would sit down and figure out a new unique way to take integers and convert them into VLCs. The resulting codes were called *universal codes*, and basically, they assigned positive integers into binary variable-length codewords. Typically, universal codes follow the rule that the smaller the number, the fewer bits it's given, under the assumption that smaller integers were more frequent than larger ones.

These VLCs could assign bit lengths in very different ways. For example, one code might add a single bit for each integer value, so that 1 = 1 bit, 2 = 2 bits, 8 = 8 bits, and so on. Or there can be sharp changes so that 1 = 1 bits, 2 = 5 bits, and 8 = 12 bits.

This is because each VLC assumes a specific probability of symbol distribution. If the Nth symbol is two times more probable than the Nth + 1 symbol, it should have one less bit. Where, if the Nth, N + 1, N + 2, N + 3 symbols are all somewhat equally probable, you might want all of them to have codewords of equal length. So, each of the VLCs we are going to introduce is associated with an ideal probability distribution, and thus better for data sets whose probabilities match that distribution closely.

As such, we list the ideal probability for most of the VLCs we are going to discuss, but note that it's interesting but not super-mega-important to know, so we are not going to explain it in detail.

It's worth noting that universal codes are a specific class of prefix codes. There are other types of VLC codes such as *uniquely decodable codes* or *nonsingular codes*, just to throw the names at you. (We don't specifically talk about those codes in this book using those terms, but note that they are represented because each prefix code is uniquely decodable and nonsingular.)

Binary code

We introduced binary code in Chapter 2 and hope you haven't forgotten everything since then, because binary code is ubiquitous in computing and thus always the end result of compression.

After Peter Elias, it is customary to denote the standard binary representation of the integer n by $B(n)$. This representation is considered the *beta* or *binary* code, and it does not satisfy the prefix property. For example, the binary representation of $2 = 10_2$ is also the prefix of $4 = 100_2$.

Now, given a set of integers between 0 and n, we can represent each in $1 + floor(\log_2(n))$ bits; that is, we can use a fixed-length representation to get around the prefix issue, as long as we're provided the value n in advance. In other words, if we know how many numbers we need to represent, we can easily determine how many bits that requires. However, if we don't know the number of distinct integers in the set in advance, we cannot use a fixed-length representation.

Meet Peter Elias

Professor Peter Elias (*http://en.wikipedia.org/wiki/Peter_Elias*) was born on November 23, 1923, in New Brunswick, New Jersey, the son of an engineer in Thomas A. Edison's laboratory (*http://www.genealogy.ams.org/id.php?id=64297*).

He attended Swarthmore College for two years before transferring to MIT in 1942 (*http://newsoffice.mit.edu/2001/elias*). Upon receiving his B.S. in business and engineering management in 1944, he enlisted in the United States Navy and served as a radio technician instructor. After he was discharged in 1946 with the rank of electronic technician's mate first class, he earned an M.A., a M.Eng and Sci., and a Ph.D. from Harvard University. He was a member of the MIT faculty from 1953 to 1991, at which time he assumed emeritus rank and became a senior lecturer.

Elias was a real bigwig when it comes to error-correcting codes (which are not covered in this book). In 1955, he introduced *convolutional codes* (*http://en.wikipedia.org/wiki/Convolutional_code*) as an alternative to *block codes* (*http://en.wikipedia.org/wiki/Block_code*). He also established the *binary erasure channel* (*http://en.wikipedia.org/wiki/Binary_erasure_channel*) and proposed *list decoding* (*http://en.wikipedia.org/wiki/List_decoding*) of error-correcting codes as an alternative to *unique decoding* (*http://en.wikipedia.org/wiki/Decoding_methods*). If you want some heavy reading before dinner, taking a look at his original work is highly recommended. (It's also fascinating.)

Unary codes

Unary coding represents a positive integer, n, with $n - 1$ ones followed by a zero. For example, 4 is encoded as 1110.[2] The length of a unary code for the integer n, is therefore n bits.

It's easy to see that the unary code satisfies the prefix property, so you can use it as a variable-length code.

The length of the codewords grows linearly by 1 for increasing numbers n, such that L is always equal to n. In binary, the number of numbers we can represent with each additional bit grows exponentially by $2n$. (Remember those 2^1, 2^2, etc. columns?)

---

2 Note, you could flip the bits here, if you wanted, and make it 0001. The basic idea is that some bit is used as the value, and the other bit is used as the delimiter.

As such, this code works best when you use it on a data set for which each symbol is twice as probable as the previous. (So, A is two times more frequent than B, which is two times more frequent than C.). Or, if you like math, we can say: in cases for which the input data consists of integers N with exponential probabilities $P(n) \sim 2^{-n}$: 1/2, 1/4, 1/8, 1/16, 1/32, and so on.

Here is an example of simple unary encoding with ideal probabilities.

Number	Code	Ideal probability
0	• (not representable)	
1	0	0.5
2	10	0.25
3	110	0.125
4	1110	0.0625

To decode unary encoding, simply read and count value bits from the stream until you hit a delimiter. Add one and output that number.

Elias gamma encoding

Elias gamma encoding is used most commonly for encoding integers whose upper bound cannot be determined beforehand; that is, we don't know what the largest number is going to be.

The main idea is that instead of encoding the integer directly, we prefix it with an encoded representation of its order of magnitude. This creates a codeword comprising two sections, the largest power of two that fits into the integer plus the remainder, like so:

1. Find the largest integer N, such that $2^N < n < 2^{N+1}$ and write $n = 2^N + L$ (where $L = n - 2^N$).

2. Encode N in unary.

3. Append L as an N-bit number to this representation. (This is really important because this symmetry is what allows us to decode the string later.)

For example, let's encode the number $n = 12$:

1. N is 3, because 2^3 is 8, and 2^4 is 16, so that $8 < 12 < 16$.

2. L is thus $12 - 8 = 4$.

3. $N = 3$ in unary is 110.

4. $L = 4$ in binary written with 3 bits is 100.

5. So, our concatenated output is 110100.

To encode a slightly larger number, let's say 42:

1. N is 5, because 2^5 is 32, and $32 < 42 < 64$.
2. L is thus $42 - 32 = 10$.
3. $N = 5$ in unary is 11110.
4. $L = 10$ written in 5 bits is 01010.
5. So, our final output is 1111001010.

Elias gamma coding, like simple unary encoding, is ideal for applications for which the probability of n is $P(N) = 1/(2n^2)$.

Here is a table with some example Elias gamma codes (note the L part in italics).

n	$2^N + L$	Code
1	2^0+0	0
2	2^1+0	10*1*
8	2^3+0	110*000*
12	2^3+4	110*100*
42	2^5+10	1111001010

Decoding Elias gamma is also straightforward:

1. Let's take the number 12, which we encoded as 110*100*.
2. Read values until we get to the delimiter: 1, 1, 0. This gives us $N = 3$.
3. Read 3 more bits 1,0,0 and convert from binary, which gives us $L = 4$.
4. Combine $2^N + L = 2^3 + 4 = 12$.

Elias delta coding

Elias delta is another variation on the same theme. In this code, Elias prepends the length in binary, making this code slightly more complex.

It works like this:

1. Write your original number, n, in binary.
2. Count the bits in binary n, and convert that count to binary, which gives us C.
3. Remove the leftmost bit of binary n, which is always one and thus can be implied.

4. Prepend the count C, in binary, to what is left of n after its leftmost bit has been removed.

5. Subtract 1 from the length of the count of C and prepend that number of zeros to the code.

For example, let's again encode the number n = 12:

1. Write n = 12 in binary, which is n = 1100.

2. The binary version of 12 has 4 bits, and converted to binary, that is C = 100.

3. Remove the leftmost bit of n = 1100, leaving you with 100.

4. Prepend C = 100 to what's left of n, which is 100, giving you 100100.

5. Subtract 1 from the length of C, 3 − 1 = 2, and prepend that many zeros to the code, giving you a final encoding of 00100100 for 12.

Elias delta is ideal for data for which n occurs with a probability of $1/[2n(\log_2(2n))^2]$.

Here is a table with some example Elias delta codings:

n in decimal	$2^N + L$	Code
1	2^0+0	0
2	2^1+0	0100
8	2^3+0	00100000
12	2^3+4	00100100
18	2^4+2	001010010
314	$2^8 + 58$	000100100111010

To decode Elias delta, do the following:

1. Read and count 0s until you hit 1.

2. Add 1 to the count of zeros, which gives you the length of C.

3. Read length of C many more bits, which gives you C.

4. Read C - 1 more bits, prepend 1, and convert to decimal.

Using our handy number 00100100:

1. Read and count 0s until you hit 1, which is 2 zeros.

2. Add 1, yielding a length of C = 3.

3. Read 3 more bits, giving you C = 100 = 4

4. Read 4 - 1 more bits, which is 100, and prepend 1, yielding 1100, which is 12.

If you don't believe this works, encode and decode the provided value 314 as an example.

And so many more!

So, now that you have worked your way through a couple of the simpler variable-length encoding algorithms, and get the gist of it, we need to tell you that there are literally hundreds of unique VLCs that have been created over the past 40 years, and we can't cover every single one of them in this book.

Google's VarInt

There are a few dominant issues with variable-length codes that keep them from being used outside of compressed data-stream representations:

- They don't align to byte/word/integer boundaries.
- For large values of n, they tend to grow past $\log_2(n)$ bits in order to be decodable.
- They are slow to decode (one bit read at a time).

For systems that deal with a great load of large integers, this makes VLCs impossible to use. However, during the early 2000s, a model of variable-length integers became a popular solution in search engines and other massive-data systems. Although it was popularized by Google (*http://goo.gl/trqn7J*) as VarInt, the basic concept was first described back in 1972,[3] and was reintroduced as "escaping for compressed integers" in 2010.

VarInt is a method of serializing integers using one or more bytes. Smaller values take fewer bytes, and larger values, of course, take more.

The process works by stringing together byte values and using the most significant bit (MSB) as a Boolean flag to denote whether it's the last byte needed to represent the number. As such, the lower 7 bits of each byte are used to store the *two's complement representation* (*http://bit.ly/29Hb2qN*) of the number. Let's take a look at this.

The number 1 can be encoded as a single byte, so its MSB is not set:

00000001

However, the value 300 is a bit more complicated.

10101100 00000010

---

3 L. Thiel and H. Heaps, "Program Design for Retrospective Searches on Large Data Bases," *Information Storage and Retrieval* 1972; 8(1):1–20

How do you determine that this is 300?

First, you drop the MSB from each byte, as this is just there to tell us whether we've reached the end of the number (as you can see, it's set in the first byte because there is more than one byte in the VarInt):

10101100 00000010

→ 0101100 0000010

Next, you reverse the order of the two groups of 7 bits because VarInts store numbers with the least significant group first. Convert to decimal. Done.

The VarInt method represents a nice hybrid approach between the flexibility of VLCs, and the efficiency of modern architectures. It lets you represent a variable integer range, but it also aligns itself with performance to decode. Double win!

Finding the Right Code for Your Data Set

The biggest difference between the codes we introduced is that each of these code sets behaves differently, given their expectation of the frequency distribution of the symbols.

So, when choosing a VLC code for your data set, you first must consider its size and range, and calculate the probabilities of its symbols. If you don't do that, encoding your data might end up not only not compressing it—you might actually end up with a much larger stream.

To get a sense of how different this is, per code, the following table shows that for a given symbol, and a probability matching each of the encodings, how many bits per symbol are needed.

Number of symbols	Elias gamma Number of bits needed for a probability distribution matching each encoding $1 / (2n^2)$	Elias delta $1 / [2n(\log_2(2n))^2]$	Elias omega[a] Largest encoded value is not known ahead of time, and small values are much more frequent than large values
1	1	1	2
2	3	4	3
3	3	4	4
8–15	7	8	6–7
64–88	13	11	10
100	13	11	11
1000	19	16	16

Number of symbols	Elias gamma	Elias delta	Elias omega[a]
	Number of bits needed for a probability distribution matching each encoding $1 / (2n^2)$	$1 / [2n(\log_2(2n))^2]$	Largest encoded value is not known ahead of time, and small values are much more frequent than large values

[a] More information on Elias omega (*https://en.wikipedia.org/wiki/Elias_omega_coding*).

What You Need to Remember

VLCs assign bits to codewords based upon the expected frequency of occurrence of a value. As such, each VLC is built with its own expectation as to how the probabilities of symbols are distributed in the data set. The trick, then, is finding the right VLC, the one that's built with a statistical model that matches your data. If you diverge from that, you'll end up with a bloated data stream.

For the first 15 or so years of information theory, compression technology was completely limited to VLCs. Basically, to compress a data set, an engineer would need to find the right code to match their set, and use it appropriately.

Thankfully, this isn't how things are done anymore.

In the next chapter, we are going to talk about how you can generate your very own VLCs using nothing but sticky notes and a pen.

CHAPTER 5

Statistical Encoding

Statistically Compressing to Entropy

A variable-length code (VLC) takes a given symbol from your input stream and assigns it a codeword that has a variable number of bits. When you apply this to a long-enough data set, you end up with an average bit-stream length that is close to the entropy of the data set—as long as the probability of your symbol distribution matches the probability table of the encoding scheme you used to build your VLC.

But let's clear something up: apart from a few situations, the VLCs discussed in Chapter 4 aren't used much in the mainstream compression world. As we mentioned in that chapter, each code is built making different assumptions about the statistical probabilities of each symbol.

Consider the chaos of using these VLCs in the real world: you're given an arbitrary data set, and you need to pick the best VLC to encode it, such that the final stream is close to the entropy size. Picking the wrong code for your data set can be disastrous, as you might end up with a compressed data stream that is bigger than the original!

So, you'd need to calculate your stream's symbol probabilities and then test against all the known VLC codes to determine which one best matches the symbol distribution for your data set. And even then, there's a chance that your data set might have a probability distribution that doesn't match exactly with an existing VLC.[1]

The answer to this is a class of algorithms called *statistical encoders*, which, instead of mapping a specific integer to a specific codeword, take the probability of your set and

---

1 Of course, where explicit VLCs *are* used in modern compressors is where the probabilities of the transformed input stream is pretty known. As such, the encoder and decoder can just agree on what VLC to use, and move forward.

use that to define new, unique variable-length codewords for your output stream. The result is that, given any input data, you can uniquely construct a custom set of code-words for it, rather than trying to match an existing VLC.

A more accurate way to describe these algorithms might be that "they excel at using the symbol probability in a data set to encode it as close to entropy as possible."

Wait, I Thought This Was Called "Entropy Coding"?

It's worth pointing out that you'll sometimes hear "entropy coding" used to describe these statistical types of compression algorithms (Wikipedia (*https://en.wikipedia.org/wiki/Entropy_encoding*) being a notable example).

Although the term entropy coding is nowadays interchangeable with "statistical coding," historically, the term has been muddled and misused in academia.

The first time that entropy coding legitimately appears might be a paper by O'Neal (1967) that stated the following:

> *Therefore, the technique of entropy coding (also called "Shannon–Fano coding" or "Huffman coding") can be used either to increase the [signal-to-noise ratio] for a given bit rate or to decrease the bit rate for a given ratio.*

In 1971, the same author published an article that has "entropy coding" in the paper title. The text contains the plural: "*entropy coding techniques (Huffman or Shannon–Fano coding)*." But sadly, no reference to a previous usage or specific definition is given.

O'Neal was trying to group together coders that used statistics to assign VLCs under a single umbrella (which makes sense) but never exactly said that much. However, from 1972 onward, many papers contain the term "entropy coding," but problematically didn't follow O'Neal's implicitly suggested definition.

For example, ITU (*http://bit.ly/29H9QDK*) recommendation H.82 (ITU-T, 1993) (*https://goo.gl/Ge6hhA*) defines an entropy coder to be "any lossless method for compressing or decompressing data." This is a bad definition, because it could be used to describe transforms such as *LZ77* (*http://bit.ly/29Hb8ij*), a *dictionary encoder* (which we cover later in this book).

In summary, entropy coding doesn't seem a clearly defined or distinguished concept, so for the sake of clarity, this book avoids using the term for anything at all. We use the term statistical encoding to define an algorithm that uses the frequency of symbols in a stream as a data point in assigning variable numbers of bits to symbols in that stream, resulting in a smaller, compressed output.

Still note, however, that many folks will use statistical encoding and entropy encoding interchangeably. When they do, feel free to positively correct them on the ambiguity of the vocabulary (it's a great conversation starter...for intense nerds).

Huffman Coding

After all that heavy talk about symbol probabilities that match specific distribution patterns, we now return to real life and, yes, sticky notes. If you do all the tedious work and the probability distribution of symbols in your data stream matches up with any good existing compression algorithm, and there are hundreds of these, you are in luck.

But what if not?

Well, that's when you need to build your very own. And to produce small, custom VLCs for a given data set, you need an algorithm that takes a list of probabilities and produces codewords.

Enter *Huffman coding*.

Huffman coding is probably the most straightforward and best-known way to build custom VLCs. Given a set of symbols and their frequencies of occurrence, the method constructs a set of variable-length codewords with the shortest average length for the symbols. It works by setting up a *decision tree* where the data is sorted and then (we're almost back to *20 Questions* again!) you record the yes/no decisions that get you down the "branches" of the tree to the "leaves"—the individual symbol you're looking for.

Shannon–Fano

Although it's not relevant to most modern systems, Shannon–Fano coding (*http://bit.ly/29H9Un6*) was one of the first techniques for constructing VLCs based on symbols and their probabilities. The reason that it's not relevant is that it doesn't achieve the lowest possible expected codeword length, but it does get pretty close. Although Shannon first proposed this technique in 1948, he attributed it to Robert Fano, who later went on to publish it officially as a technical report.

As an example, the PKZIP/IMPLODE format (*https://en.wikipedia.org/wiki/PKZIP*) ignores using Huffman encoding, and instead, chooses two to three Shannon–Fano trees.

Building a Huffman Tree

In summary, Huffman discovered that if he used a binary tree, he could use the probabilities from the symbol table alongside the branches of the binary tree to create an optimal binary code.

Here's a tiny—and incomplete—example table:

Symbol	Frequency of occurrence
A	4
B	1
C	1

So, let's put these on sticky notes, sort them by probability, and call them the leaves of the binary Huffman tree that we are going to build from the bottom up (see Figure 5-1).

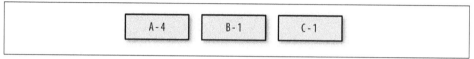

Figure 5-1. The starter nodes sorted by their frequency of occurrence.

First, take the two symbols with the smallest probabilities, move them one level deeper, and create a parent that is a combination of the two symbols and their probabilities, as depicted in Figure 5-2.

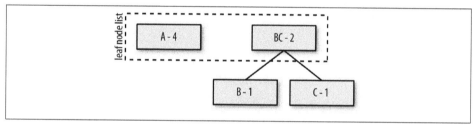

Figure 5-2. Creating a combined parent node for B and C.

Second, repeat this process for the remaining A and combine it with BC to create the new root ABC, which represents our complete set of symbols (see Figure 5-3).

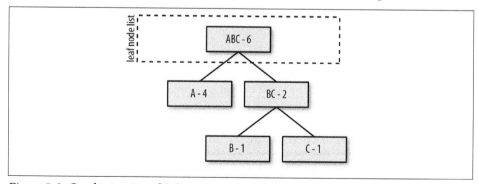

Figure 5-3. Combining A and BC to create the ABC root tree.

Generating Codewords

To set up the tree for generating codewords, assign 0s to all left branches, and 1s to all right branches (Figure 5-4).

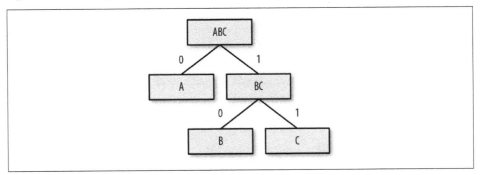

Figure 5-4. Assigning 0s and 1s to the branches.

Finally, to find a code for a given symbol/leaf node, "walk the tree" from the top down,[2] and line up the 1s and 0s from most significant bit (MSB) to least significant bit (LSB)—that is, left to right.

For example, to determine the code for B, start at the root, traverse to the right (1), then to the left (0), resulting in 10 as the encoded representation (Figure 5-5).

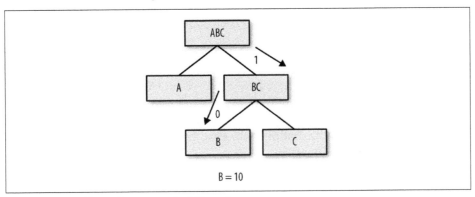

Figure 5-5. Walking the tree to find B's code.

Finally, repeat this same process for all the remaining symbols/leaves of the tree (Figure 5-6).

---

2 Guilty admission: this isn't entirely accurate. The traditional Huffman code works by traversing bottom up (as opposed to the Shannon–Fano method, which works from the top down). For programmers: in practice, we've found that traversing top-down yields a more efficient code-wise implementation, because it's simpler to keep child pointers and tree traversals that way.

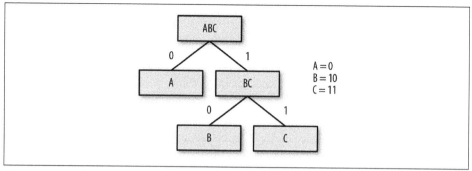

Figure 5-6. Codes for all symbols (leaf nodes) in the tree.

Encoding and Decoding

Congratulations! You now have constructed a VLC assignment for your unique data set, which you can use to encode your data. Walk through the input stream, and for each symbol, write the appropriate codeword to the output.

As with other VLCs, for decoding purposes, you need to transfer the symbol-to-codeword table along with your compressed content and mirror the standard VLC decoding process

Because creating the tree takes more "effort" (uses compute resources) than passing the symbol-to-codeword table (increases data stream size), you should always prepend your data stream with the codeword table, not re-create it at the destination.[3]

Practical Implementations

Folks have done a crazy amount of amazing analysis on Huffman codes over the past 50 years or so, and have come up with variants to ensure that they operate within some performance or memory threshold, or produce various codes that are skewed toward a specific probability. Entire books have been written about this algorithm and its complexity and optimizations.

---

3 Balancing data transmission with computing resources is a theme we'll return to at the end of this book; it's a recurrent challenge.

But that's all we're going to say about it—you've got enough of the mechanics to understand how your data is interacting with algorithms when you begin to try them.

Meet David Huffman

David Albert Huffman (August 9, 1925–October 7, 1999) was a pioneer in computer science, known for his Huffman coding (*http://bit.ly/29HbaH3*).[4]

In 1951, David A. Huffman and his classmates in an electrical engineering graduate course on information theory were given the choice of a term paper or a final exam. For the term paper, Huffman's professor, Robert M. Fano, had assigned what at first appeared to be a simple problem. Students were asked to find the most efficient method of representing numbers, letters, or other symbols using a binary code. Besides being a nimble intellectual exercise, finding such a code would make it possible for information to be compressed for transmission over a computer network, or for storage in a computer's memory.

Huffman worked on the problem for months, developing a number of approaches, but none that he could prove to be the most efficient. Finally, he despaired of ever reaching a solution and decided to begin studying for the final. Just as he was throwing his notes in the garbage, the solution came to him. "It was the most singular moment of my life," Huffman says. "There was the absolute lightning of sudden realization."[5]

That epiphany added Huffman to the legion of largely anonymous engineers whose innovative thinking forms the technical underpinnings for the accoutrements of modern living—in his case, from facsimile machines to modems and a myriad other devices. "Huffman code is one of the fundamental ideas that people in computer science and data communications are using all the time," says Donald E. Knuth of Stanford University, who is the author of the multivolume series *The Art of Computer Programming* (Addison-Wesley, 1997).

Like so many other early breakthroughs, Huffman might never have found this solution without the help of his professor, Fano, who noted that Claude Shannon had also struggled with the same issue. "It was my luck to be there at the right time, and also not have my professor discourage me by telling me that other good people had struggled with this problem," Huffman says.

---

4 He was also one of the pioneers in the field of mathematical origami (*http://goo.gl/288I0W*), the wonders of which you can begin exploring with Robert Lang's TED talk "The Math and Magic of Origami" (*https://goo.gl/3jv5xg*).

5 Inna Pivkina, "Discovery of Huffman Codes" (*http://bit.ly/297Nzv5*).

Arithmetic Coding

The Huffman method is simple, efficient, and produces the best codes for individual data symbols. However, it doesn't always produce the most effective codewords for a given set.

In fact, the only case for which Huffman produces ideal VLCs (codes whose average size equals the entropy) is when the symbols occur at probabilities that are negative powers of 2 (i.e., numbers such as 1/2, 1/4, or 1/8). This is because the Huffman method assigns a codeword with an integer number of bits to each symbol in the given symbol set.

Information theory shows that a symbol with probability 0.4 should ideally be assigned a 1.32-bit code, because $-\log_2(0.4) \approx 1.32$. The Huffman method, however, assigns such a symbol a code of 1 or 2 bits.

Sadly, as long as the number of bits we assign to a codeword are integer-based, there will always be a bloated difference between the number of encoded bits and the actual bits required by entropy. So, to fix that, we must move away from assigning integer-based codewords to symbols at a 1:1 ratio.

This is where *arithmetic coding* comes in. Rather than assigning codewords to symbols in a 1:1 fashion, this algorithm transforms the entire input stream from a set of symbols to one (excessively long) numeric value, whose $\log_2$ representation is closer to the true value of entropy for the stream.

The magic of arithmetic compression is a transform that it applies to the source data in order to create a single output number, which takes fewer bits to represent than the source data itself.

Story Time: Where Arithmetic Coding Originated

Peter Elias first proposed the concept behind arithmetic compression in the early 1960s. But, it wasn't until a decade later that Jorma Rissanen from IBM published some of the first suitable research for its implementation—alongside a massive patent.

As a result, for the next couple of decades, arithmetic compression pretty much fell off the map, due to an impossibly aggressive patent strategy enforced by IBM. The patent problem was so enormous and arithmetic compression so good, a different algorithm called *Range Coding* (https://en.wikipedia.org/wiki/Range_encoding) was invented in 1979. It basically did the same thing as arithmetic compression but was free from patents.

In the early 2000s, the patent finally expired. Arithmetic compression took off again and achieved status as the gold standard for the current generation of statistical encoders.

In fact, the majority of modern compression formats for archives (such as LZMA (*http://bit.ly/28KCeka*) and BZIP (*https://en.wikipedia.org/wiki/Bzip2*)) and audio and video (such as JPEG (*https://en.wikipedia.org/wiki/JPEG*), WebP (*https://en.wikipedia.org/wiki/WebP*), webM (*https://en.wikipedia.org/wiki/WebM*), and H.264 (*https://en.wikipedia.org/wiki/H.264/MPEG-4_AVC*)) all work with an arithmetic compression system as their statistical encoding step.

Finding the Right Number

Arithmetic coding works by transforming a single string into a number that requires fewer bits to represent than the original string. For example, "TOBEORNOT" could be represented by 236712^6, whose ceil($-\log_2(236712)$) = 18 bits. Compare this with the ASCII version of "TOBEORNOT," which sits at 56 bits.

But this isn't as easy as just picking a number at random, as we did earlier. Arithmetic coding goes through a complex process of calculating this number from an input stream. The trick is that choosing the number is actually a modification on the binary search algorithm that we introduced in Chapter 2 (you know, the chapter you were not supposed to skip).

If you recall from that chapter, you can use a binary search to output 0/1 bits to catalog the search's no/yes decision process as we were checking whether a number fit into one of two spaces against a pivot value. But what if we had four spaces? Each decision would then output 2 bits (for one-fourth of the number range, respectively). Still makes pretty good sense, right?

Arithmetic coding kinda works along this path, but with some serious modifications.

Arithmetic coding creates a number space $[0,1)^7$ and subdivides it based on the probability of symbols in the data stream. So, "A" would be given [0,0.25) if its probability were 25%, and B, with a probability of 10%, would then be given [0.25,0.35), and so on, as shown here:

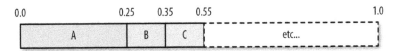

When the encoder reads a symbol, it finds the range for that symbol. For example, if A were read, the range [0.0,0.25) would be used. After a symbol is read, the encoder

---

6 It actually isn't. This is just an example number to show you the general steps.

7 The [0,1) notation indicates that the number 0 is included in the range, and 1 is not, making the range 0 through 0.99999…, with as many 9s as you need.

will subdivide that symbol range and assign new range values for symbols proportionally.

For example, if our stream provided three A symbols in a row, the encoder would subdivide the A range three times, as illustrated here:

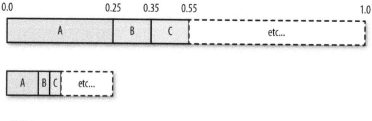

Basically, each symbol recursively divides its range until we reach the end of the input stream. After that's done, we have a final range of values, such as [0.253212, 0.25421). The number you output, is a value in this range. So for our example, for an input string of AAA, the output could be anything in the range [0,0.015625).

Encoding

Let's encode a complete example with three symbols, R, G, and B, with respective probabilities of 0.4, 0.5, and 0.1. We assign them ranges in the interval [0,1) according to their probability, as shown in the following table (note that the entropy of this table is 1.36):

Symbol	Probability	Interval
R	0.4	[0,0.4)
G	0.5	[0.4,0.9)
B	0.1	[0.9,1)

The following diagram shows the same information represented in number-line form of the ranges for three symbols, R, G, and B:

Using this probability setup, let's encode the string "GGB."

The first symbol we read from the input stream is "G." Because the interval of G, according to our table, is [0,4,0.9), we subdivide the number space between the values of 0.4 and 0.9 according to probabilities, which gives us a new range of intervals, as shown in the updated figure and table that follow.

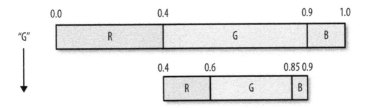

Symbol	Probability	Updated interval
R	0.4	[0.4,0.6)
G	0.5	[0.6,0.85)
B	0.1	[0.85,0.9)

We now read the second symbol from the input stream. It's another G, so we again subdivide the G range of numbers, which is between 0.6 and 0.85, and update the intervals as shown in the following figure and the table.

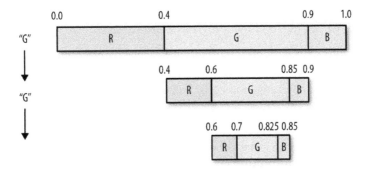

Symbol	Probability	Updated interval
R	0.4	[0.6,0.7)
G	0.5	[0.7,0.825)
B	0.1	[0.825,0.85)

And finally, we read and subdivide again for the letter B, and update the figure and table once more.

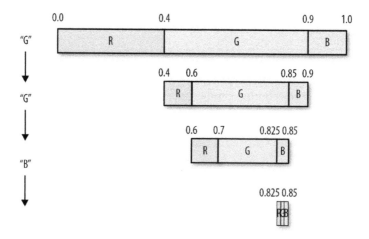

Symbol	Probability	Updated interval
R	0.4	[0.825,0.835)
G	0.5	[0.835,0.8475)
B	0.1	[0.8475,0.85)

Congratulations! You just arithmetically encoded a stream!

Picking the Right Output Value

So, we've subdivided the range intervals, but what number do we output as the final result?

Our final interval for B is [0.825,0.85), and any number from that range will serve the purpose of letting us reconstruct the original string, giving us some choices between 0.825 and 0.849999.... This being a book about compression, we want to use the number that we can represent with the fewest bits (and as close to our 1.36 bits entropy goal) as possible.

The number in this range that requires the fewest bit is 0.83.

Finally, because the decoder "knows" that this is a floating-point number, we can drop the leading 0 for additional savings and end up with 83, which with $\log_2(83) = 7$ bits, gives us 1.42 bits per symbol, which is almost at entropy.

Decoding

Decoding from this final number is pretty straightforward—basically the encoding process in reverse. Just as with encoding, we begin by creating the segmented range between [0,1) based on the probabilities, as demonstrated here:

We then take our input value, 83, add the leading "0" to get 0.83, and find which interval it falls into. We output the symbol associated with that interval.

In our case, 0.83 falls in the range 0.4,0.9, giving us the value G to output.

We then subdivide the G space according to the probabilities (same as when we were encoding).

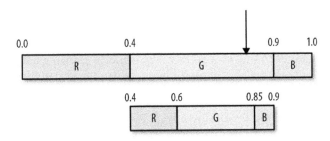

To get our second symbol, we repeat the process. Our input value is still 0.83, which falls (again) in G's range, so we output another G, and subdivide again, as shown here:

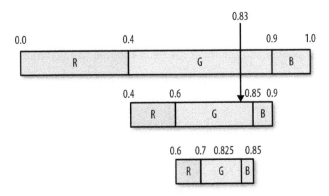

Continuing one more time, 0.83 falls in the range 0.825,0.85, which is the range for the symbol B, so we output B.

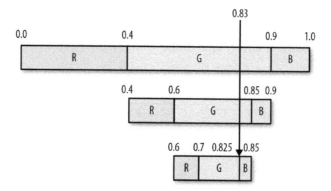

This gives us our final decoded stream as GGB.

Pretty nifty, eh? Our decoding process basically works by drawing a line through each recursive space and outputting whatever symbol we land in at that time.

How Subdividing the Range Intervals Based on Probability Results in Compression

As an initial state, let's subdivide our space between [0,1) evenly among 10 values. This is equivalent to an input stream for which all symbols have equal probabilities.

Then, we read a symbol and subdivide the space between [0.2,0.3) into 10 equal buckets, as well.

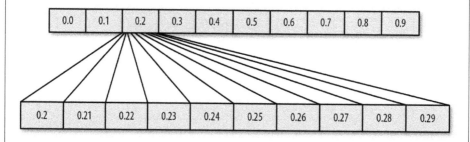

Now, let's pause for a second. At this point, we've read in a single symbol. If we stopped encoding at this point, we'd be selecting a number in the 0.2x range and our output would be two digits long.

As this pattern continues, each subdivision adds another digit to our final output number. So a third subdivision would give us 0.*XXX*, and a fourth 0.*XXXX*, as shown here:

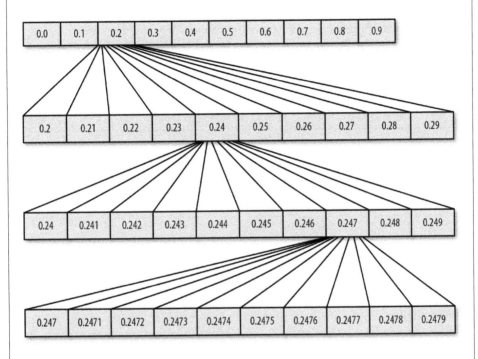

The problem with this is that because each subdivision adds more digits to the output, we end up with one extra digit for each symbol read.

However, even with this, we can already achieve compression. For example, if we're reading in ASCII data, each symbol uses 8 bits, but each subdivision only adds $-\log_2(10)$, which rounds to ~3.3 bits to our output number (because it's increasing by a power of 10 at each step).

But we can do better.

Rather than subdividing the space evenly, let's give some spaces more size. Suppose that the first space goes from [0,91) and the other 9 spaces are crammed between [0.91,1). This is equivalent to an input stream for which one symbol is seriously more probable than the other nine.

After reading the first symbol, we subdivide the space between [0.0,0.9), keeping our same weighting, as shown here:

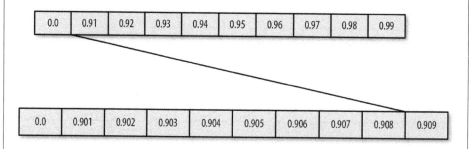

So, if we stopped encoding at this point, we'd have the ability to have either a one-digit number "0" or a three-digit number "90x." And if we assign the one-digit number range to our most probable symbol, we gain enormous savings—bingo!

Improving Decoding Performance

Now, for you performance buffs out there, it's worth pointing out that the illustrated decoding process might not be as performant as you'd like. If you have a 1 MB stream, you're going to need to subdivide your interval, each time, into as many separate subsections as you have unique symbols. That can be a lot of floating-point math and division.

Here's an alternate way to do this: rather than subdividing the space, remove the spaces' influence from our code.

For example, given our previous frequency and intervals table, and the final output value 83, we can set up our number interval.

We begin by setting our input number to 0.83, which falls in the interval of 0.4 and 0.9, so we know the first output symbol is G.

But now, we need to remove the influence of the first symbol G from our number. We do this by subtracting the lower limit of G (0.4) from 0.83, and dividing the interval by the width of G (0.5)—the result number is 0.86, as demonstrated here:

$(0.83-0.4) / 0.5 = 0.86$

Now we continue. 0.86 which falls in the interval of 0.4 and 0.9, so we know the next output symbol is G. We output that, and then we remove the influence of the second G from the number. We do this by subtracting the lower limit of G (0.4) from 0.86, and dividing the interval by the width of G (0.5), the result number is 0.92.

(0.86 − 0.4) / 0.5 = 0.92

0.92 sits between 0.9 and 1.0, which we know is the value of B.

We can output that to the stream, and we're done.

Practical Implementations

The adoption and dominance of arithmetic coding since its patent expiration in the 2000s has led to a plethora of topics that relate to practical implementations of this algorithm. More impressive is how many of them have been modified for specific *codecs*, such as the binary-only versions used by JPG (*https://en.wikipedia.org/wiki/JPEG*) and H.264 (*https://en.wikipedia.org/wiki/H.264/MPEG-4_AVC*) codecs. Those *lossy compression* methods are out of scope for this book, but there are plenty of resources (*http://www.cc.gatech.edu/~jarek/courses/7491/Arithmetic2.pdf*) out there if you'd like to investigate more.

Asymmetric Numeral Systems

After a 40-year battle between Huffman and arithmetic encodings, it would seem as though both might have been usurped by a brand new class of statistical encoder.

In 2007, Jarek Duda presented a new information theory concept called *asymmetric numeral systems* (*http://arxiv.org/abs/1311.2540*) (ANS) that had direct relations to data compression. Effectively, ANS is a new approach to accurate entropy coding, which can get arbitrarily close to optimal Shannon entropy, provides compression ratios similar to arithmetic coding, and has performance similar to Huffman coding.

Although Jarek Duda's papers detail a lot of cool mathematical revelations, you can apply the algorithm itself much like other statistical encoders:[8]

1. A numerical space is subdivided based on symbol frequencies.
2. A table is created, which maps subspaces to discrete integer values.

---

8 Especially the tANS variant, which is designed to be a direct replacement to Huffman encoding. See the paper "The Use of Asymmetric Numeral Systems as an Accurate Replacement for Huffman Coding" (*http://goo.gl/D9DW88*) or "Asymmetric Numeral Systems: Entropy Coding Combining Speed of Huffman Coding with Compression Rate of Arithmetic Coding" (*http://arxiv.org/abs/1311.2540*).

3. Each symbol is processed by reading and responding to values in the table.
4. Variable bits are written to the output stream.

The two parts that are unique to this algorithm are in step 2 (the table) and step 4 (variable bits).

So, let's take a look at those more closely.

Encoding and Decoding Using a Transform Table

The tANS variant of ANS works by moving around a table of values.

As an example, let's just assume that you're given the table that follows. Ignore how we've created it, we'll get to table creation in a moment.

State/row	A	B	C
1	2	3	5
2	4	6	10
3	7	8	15
4	9	11	20
5	12	14	25
6	13	17	30
7	16	21	
8	18	22	
9	19	26	
10	23	28	
11	24		
12	27		
13	29		
14	31		

Given the preceding table, let's walk through how to encode the input string BAA:

1. Given an input stream BAA, we begin with a pair of [row index, input symbol], which is [1,B].[9]

2. We use this pair to reference a location in the table from which to read our next value. We grab the value at cell [1,B] in the table, which is 3, and make that our new row index for [3,?].

---

9 Worth noting that 1 is always the initial state.

---

3. To get the column index, we then read the next symbol, which is A, completing the new table index [3,A].

4. Again, we grab the value at that cell in the table, which is 7.

5. We read the next symbol, which is also A, we end up with [7,A].

6. And the value at that index is 16.

7. We can continue forward with this until we hit the end of the table (or the end of the string).

8. The transform of this table takes BAA and results in [3,7,16].

Decoding works in the exact opposite way.

1. We begin with the last value, 16.

2. We then search the entire table and find that 16 sits at row 7, column A.

3. We output A as our symbol and 7 becomes the new current value.

4. We search the table again and find that 7 is at row 3, column A.

5. We output A, again, and set 3 as our new value.

6. When we search for our last 3, we see that it's at row 1, column B. Because we're in row 1, we know we can't move further, so we're done decoding.

7. The decoded stream is [A,A,B] because we were decoding the list from *back* to *front*.

8. Our last step is to reverse to get to the original BAA.

You can see that this table lets us encode an input string and decode it properly, given a nifty way to move around it.

Creating the Reference Table

The core of this algorithm is the magical reference table, which makes it possible for these types of transforms to occur. The table itself is created by first assigning each symbol a column in the table, such that the symbols are sorted by probability, left to right from highest to lowest.

In the previous table, the symbols A, B, C have the probabilities $P([A,B,C]) = [0.45,0.35,0.2]$, and are each assigned a column of the table.

From here, we must fill in values into the table, adhering to a few specific properties:

- Every value in the table is unique (no repeats)
- Numbers in each column are sorted from lowest to highest

- Numbers in every row are larger than the number (index) of that row

If you can adhere to these principles, the encoding/decoding transform that we've shown should work just fine. But for tANS to become a true entropy encoder, there are two more properties that we must consider:

Determining the number of values in a column
> The number of values in a column is equal to the probability of the column-symbol, multiplied by maxVal.[10]

Determining the numbers in each row
> Numbers in a row are selected to align with the probability of occurrence for a symbol, such that if we divide the row-number by a value in a column, the resulting value is (roughly) equal to the probability of that column's symbol.

Let's take a closer look at these properties for our example.

The first property is somewhat straightforward. The largest value in the table is maxVal = 31. In accordance with the property, we subdivide the space of maxVal = 31, assigning $P(s)$ * maxVal numbers to each symbol-column. For our example:

- B has $P(B) = 0.35$, which results in a column that is floor(0.35 * 31) = 10 elements high.
- The same goes for C (0.2 * 31 = 6).
- However, the most-probable symbol, in the leftmost column A, has $P(A)$ * maxVal + 1 = 0.45 * 31 + 1 = 14 rows. That's because the most probable symbol adds an extra row for the maxVal.

This has the effect of subdividing the maxVal space, giving slots for each symbol, equal to its probability.[11]

The second property defines that values in a row can be calculated by multiplying the row number by the probability of each symbol.

For our example table, the probabilities for the symbols S = [A,B,C] are $P(S)$ = [0.45,0.35,0.2], and picking a row, say row 5, the values are 12, 14, 25.

When we divide those values by the row index, we get a result that's pretty close to the symbol probabilities: [5 / 12, 5 / 14 , 5 / 25] = [0.41666.,0.357,0.2] ~= $P(S)$.

This second property must remain true for all rows. You can see that for column A, each row has a value that's about right with regard to $P(A) = 0.45$.

---

10 We haven't talked about maxVal yet. We'll get into choosing the proper maxVal in a moment.

11 Note that if you're creating this as a full 2D table (rather than letting the height of each column be variable), you'll need to insert some value in the column positions greater than its column height (−1 or something) to signify that those cells are empty/invalid.

Row #	P(A)	Row #/P(A)	Actual table value	Row #/value
1	0.45	2.2223…	2	0.5
2	0.45	4.4444…	4	0.5
3	0.45	6.6666…	7	0.42
4	0.45	8.8888…	9	0.444…
5	0.45	11.1111…	12	0.416…

So, why is there sometimes a discrepancy between the assigned table value and the numerically calculated table value? It's to avoid collisions.

Each value in the table must be unique. However, because we are rounding numbers up and down, we can end up with collisions at a few spots. For example, 1 / P(C) = 5, whereas 2 / P(B) = 5.714.

We resolve collisions by iterating forward to find the next highest value that is not yet used in the table. For example, in the case of assigning a symbol to column B, for row 2 we can't use the value 5 (because it's already used in row 1), so we try the next greater value, 6, which hasn't been used in the table yet, and assign[12] that value.

By adhering to these two properties, you can create the entire preceding table that will properly encode/decode values and compress your data.

Choosing a maxVal

Choosing maxVal directly affects your compression output, which is directly related to the amount of integer precision that your encoding allows.

The goal, therefore, is to assign each symbol a subspace whose size matches the probability of the symbol itself. Now, if the encoding process and table were computed in floating-point space, this wouldn't be that big of a deal: simply assign each symbol a space equal to its frequency. However, our encode/decode works with integers. As such, we need to create an integer space of some size (between 2 and maxVal) such that we can assign subranges of it to each symbol without running into precision problems.

Suppose that your data set contains 28 unique symbols. At the bare minimum, you then need LOG2(28) = 5 bits, space size, giving you a maxVal of $2^5 - 1 = 31$.

---

12 With respect to performance, there's a bunch of different ways to accomplish this type of marking of used variables. We suggest checking out the "bingo board" method (*http://www.ezcodesample.com/abs/abs_article.html*) by Andrew Polar.

However, because not every symbol is equally probable, this doesn't give us enough space to assign different symbols different space sizes. To accommodate, this we need to increase our number of bits.

As such, choosing a maxVal should be a function of the minimum number of bits you need, plus a few extra bits to help with precision:

$$numPrecisionBits = LOG2(numSymbols) + magicExtraBits$$

$$maxVal = (2^{numPrecisionBits}) - 1$$

Where magicExtraBits is some value between 2 and 8, or whatever works for your data set. The number of magicExtraBits, as we will show in a moment, trades off quality for processing time; the higher the value, the better compression but the longer it takes to compress.

Using ANS for Compression

We previously identified how to move around our reference table; however, the output didn't result in statistical compression. To achieve compression, we need to tweak our algorithm just a tad:

- First, instead of starting with row 1, our starting state/row is going to be maxVal.
- Second, for each symbol we read from the stream:
  - Set targetRow to the column height for that symbol.
  - Bitshift the state value *right* until it is smaller than the targetRow.
  - Each bit that is dropped from state during the shift, should be output to our encoded bitstream.

Let's walk through an example encoding of the string "ABAC", given the above modifications and the table we previously presented:

1. Because the state = maxVal = 31 (binary 11111), that is what we start with.
2. Read the first symbol, which is A, giving us [31,A], and setting targetRow to 14.
3. Because 31 > 14, we start shifting and outputting bits.
   a. We shift state right once, to 1111, truncating the rightmost 1 to our output stream→**1**.
   b. State is now 15, which is still larger than 14; thus, we shift right again, making state 111 and outputting another 1 bit to the output stream. →**1**
   c. State is now 7, and we've truncated and written out two bits (11).

4. We now assign state to the table value at [7,A], which is 16 (binary 10000).

5. Read the next symbol, which is B, resulting in [16,B], and setting targetRow to 10.

6. Because 16 > 10, we start shifting and outputting bits.

   a. We shift 16 right once to set state = 8 (binary 1000), emitting a 0 to the output. →**0**

   b. Because 8 <10, we can move to the next symbol.

7. We set state to the table value at [8,B], which is 22 (binary 10110).

8. Read the next symbol, which is A, resulting in [22,A], and setting targetRow to 14.

9. Because 22 > 14, we shift and output bits. We shift right to get state = 1011, emitting 0. →**0**

10. We set state to the table value at [11,A], which is 24 (binary 11000).

11. Read the next symbol, which is C, resulting in [24,C], and targetRow to 6.

12. Because 24 > 6, we start shifting and outputting bits. We shift twice to get state = 110, emitting 00. →**0 0**

13. We set state to the table value at [6,C], which is 30 (11110).

14. Because our stream is now empty, we output our state value (11110) to the stream. →**11110**

15. Our final stream is thus: **11000011110** and 11 bits long. Plus the bits taken up by the symbol probabilities table.

Decoding Example

Decoding works in the opposite order:

1. Read in our frequency data from the compressed stream.

2. Create the table from the symbol frequency information.

3. Read a value from the stream.

4. Find its location in the table.

5. Output the column as the symbol.

6. Make value = row.

7. Read in some new bits.

It's worth noting that in this example our maxVal = 31, or 5 bits of precision.

After creating the table, we work through our encoded 11000011110 stream backward as follows:

1. Working with 5 bits for our state targeted, read the last 5 bits 11110(30) of the stream.

2. We find the only number 30 in the table at location [C,6].

3. **Output the symbol C.**

4. 6 or 110 is only 3 bits, so we need to read 2 more from the stream (always try to make 5 bits).

5. Read the last 2 bits, 00, and append them to 110, resulting in 11000 24

6. Find the only location of 24 in the table at [A,11].

7. **Output the symbol A.**

8. 11 (binary 1011) is only 4 bits, so read 1 more bit from the stream, giving you 10110 (22).

9. Find 22 in the table at [B,8].

10. **Output the symbol B.**

11. 8 (binary 1000) is only 4 bits, so read 1 more, giving you 10000 (16).

12. Find 16 in the table at [A,7].

13. **Output the symbol A.**

14. 7 (binary 111) is only 3 bits, so read 2 more, giving you 11111(31).

15. Because this value now equals our maxValue (11111), we know this to be the end-of-message marker, so we quit decoding.

16. We reverse the string and have returned to **ABAC**.

So Where Does the Compression Come From?

Compression comes from the bit-wise output.

Because the least probable symbols have shorter columns, the valid row values are farther removed (in bit distance) from the max-symbol. Therefore, more right-shifts are required to get to the lower row indexes, which means more bits are pushed to the stream for each iteration. So, less probable symbols result in more bits being output to the final stream.

As we mentioned previously, giving more bits produces a higher precision for your space (and thus, a larger maxVal). This causes the values in the reference table to have fewer precision collisions, because the larger space allows for integers to more closely match the value given by $P(s) * maxVal$. Recall that collisions in the table result in linearly searching for a larger value that hasn't been used yet. When encoding, this difference between the computed value and the actual value can result in more bit-shifts to get the state value below the target row value. When precision is high, there are fewer collisions, producing less bloat per value and fewer bits being shifted to the output stream.

The downside, though, is that larger precision produces a larger reference table, which takes significant time to create and significant amounts of memory to hold. So ensure that you find the right trade-off between performance and memory for your particular implementation.

Practical Compression: Which Statistical Algorithm Do I Choose?

So, you've got some awesome data set, and three awesome algorithms to apply statistical compression to them. Which one do you choose?

This is a common problem, and for the majority of the past 20 years, there's been a massive nerd-fight going on in the compression world between Huffman and arithmetic coding. This debate first came to light in 1993, when Bookstein and Klein published a paper called "Is Huffman Coding Dead?" (*http://bit.ly/29aVr0Y*)

Although it's been more than 20 years since that paper was released, the arguments are still held strongly by both sides of the debate.

Because computers are getting faster and faster (and the patent on arithmetic compression has expired), arithmetic compression has become the more dominantly implemented version. It has taken over in most multimedia encoders, and is even being implemented into hardware effectively.

But ANS has changed all that. In its short time in the world of compression, it has already begun to take over the majority of positions held by Huffman and arithmetic encoders for the past 20 years.

For example, the ZHuff (*http://fastcompression.blogspot.com/p/zhuff.html*), LZTurbo (*https://sites.google.com/site/powturbo/*), LZA (*http://bit.ly/29H5VXB*), Oodle and LZNA compressors (*http://www.radgametools.com/oodlecompressors.htm*) have already made the move over to ANS. Given its speed and performance, it seems only a matter of time before it will become the dominant form of encoding. In fact, in 2013, a more performance-focused version of the algorithm called Finite State Entropy (FSE) (*https://github.com/Cyan4973/FiniteStateEntropy*), which only uses additions, masks, and shifts, came onto the scene, making ANS even more attractive for developers. It's so powerful, that a Gzip-variant, dubbed LZFSE, was unveiled in 2015 as a core API in Apple's next iOS release (*http://apple.co/297T1y7*).

The road forward seems pretty clear at this point: ANS and FSE might usher the end of the decades that Huffman and arithmetic have enjoyed on the top of the charts.

CHAPTER 6

Adaptive Statistical Encoding

Locality Matters for Entropy

All the statistical encoders mentioned in Chapter 5 require an initial pass through the data to compute probabilities before encoding can start. This leaves us with a few shortcomings: you always need to do an extra pass through the data to calculate the probabilities, and after you have calculated the probabilities for the entire data set, you are stuck with those numbers. Neither of those is a problem for relatively small data sets.

However, the larger the size of the data set that you're compressing, the more bloated your statistical encoding will be with respect to entropy. This is because different subsections of the data set will have different probability characteristics. And if you're dealing with streaming data—a video or audio stream, for example—there's no "end" to the data set, so you just can't "take two passes."

These concepts, then, will apply to streaming data, but let's look at them in the context of a relatively simple example data set. The first third of your stream might contain an excessive number of Q's, whereas the last two thirds might have exactly none. The probability tables for your statistical encoder would not account for this locality. If the symbol Q has a probability of 0.01, it is expected to appear more or less evenly along the entirety of the stream; that is, about every 0.01th value would be Q.

This is not how real data works. There's always some sort of *locality-dependent skewing*[1] that bundles symbols, thoughts, or words together in subsections of your data set.

---

1 We totally made up this term.

As a consequence, the probability information that the statistical encoders are built on creates codes that are bloated with respect to entropy: they don't take into account local shifts in the statistics. If, for example, you broke up a stream into N chunks and compressed each one individually, you might end up with a smaller output than by compressing the entire input as one (if there's lots of locality-dependent skewing[2]).

Let's consider a simple example data set:

```
AAAAAAAAAAAAAAAAAAAAAABBBBBBBBBBBBBBBBCDEFGHIJKLMNOPQRSTUVWXYZ
```

This stream has an entropy of ~3.48, suggesting that we should, on average, use about 3.48 bits per symbol, and expect a final encoded size of 198.36 bits. The Huffman-encoded version of this set is about 202 bits, which puts us at about 3.54 bits per symbol,[3] which is not too shabby.

But let's be honest here. We can do better than that. We can plainly see that the first half of the stream is made up of only two characters, highly repeated. In reality, we'd love to find a way to split the stream, so that we could get better encoding for the first half of the stream. Wouldn't it be great, if instead of creating one variable-length code (VLC) for the entire stream, we could break it in half, and assign the first half 1 bit per symbol, and the second half 5 bits per symbol? The net result would be 122 bits, giving us 2.1 bits per symbol. (And just to point this out, this has us beating Shannon. In a blowout.)

This leads us to a very important place in the compression world, the concept that locality matters.[4] As data is created in a linear fashion, there's a high probability that parts of the stream will have characteristics that are completely different from other parts of the stream.

The real challenge of implementing this type of optimization is in how to optimally divide the stream. Scanning ahead as we go, and trying to find the right segments, will only lead you to madness and something that feels like an *NP-complete problem*. So, instead of trying to scan ahead and find the right split points as we are encoding, we instead allow our statistical encoders to "reset" themselves.

This process is pretty simple in concept: As we're encoding our stream, if the variance between the "expected" entropy and the "actual encoded bits" begins to diverge by a significant amount, the encoder resets the probability tables, and then continues using the reset tables.

---

2 Making up terms is fun. Using those made up terms a bunch of times is funner. We should do this more often...

3 At face value, the discrepancy between these two numbers (entropy and actual bits-per-symbol) has everything to do with the same integer patterns that we covered in Chapter 5 (the difference between Huffman and arithmetic coders, specifically).

4 Actually #PERFMATTERS, but that's a different book...

This ability of adapting to the locality of the entropy of a stream is often called a "dynamic" or "adaptive" variant of a statistical encoder. And these variants make up the majority of all important, high-performance, high-compression algorithms for most media streams, such as images, video, and audio.

Adaptive VLC Encoding

Let's look at perhaps one of the simplest versions of an adaptive algorithm, just to understand the basic workings.

Typically, there are three stages to statistical compression:[5]

1. Walk through the stream and calculate probabilities.

2. Assign variable-length codes to symbols based on their probability.

3. Walk through the stream again and output the appropriate codewords.

Basically, you do two passes through the data stream and have one VLC set for the entire set of data. The issue here is the static nature of the VLC table.

Now the *adaptive* version of this process collapses these three steps into a single, very complex, pass through the data set. The key lies in our symbol-to-codeword table not being set in stone; rather, it can update as it encounters symbols.

 The trick to adaptive statistical encoding has to do with not having a set-in-stone VLC table. Instead, the VLC is constructed on the fly as symbols are encountered. The dynamic nature of this process lets us do other stuff to the table as we see fit; like, reset it.

Dynamically Building a VLC Table

Dynamically building your VLC table follows this pattern:

As the encoder processes the data stream, for each symbol it encounters, it asks the following:

- Have we encountered this symbol yet?
    - If so, then output its currently assigned codeword, and update the probabilities.
    - If not, then do something special. (We will get to this part in a bit.)

---

5 When you talk to people who are obnoxiously smart about data compression, they typically say that statistical encoding comprises two phases: modeling and prediction. There. Are you happy now, John Brooks?

So, with that in mind, suppose that as you begin processing your stream, you've been given some expected probabilities and symbols to start with. As such, you currently have a VLC table that looks like this:

Symbol	Probability	Code
A	0.5	0
B	0.4	10
C	0.1	11

Now, let's read the next symbol off the input stream, which happens to be the symbol B:

1. Output the currently assigned codeword for B, which is 10.

2. Update the probabilities table because B has just become a little bit more probable (and the other symbols a little bit less).

Symbol	Updated probability	Code
A	0.45	0
B	0.45	10
C	0.1	11

3. The next symbol is a B again, so we output a 10 again, and update our probabilities.

Symbol	Updated probability	Updated code
A	0.4	10
B	0.5	0
C	0.1	11

Notice the important thing that happened here. Because B has become the most probable symbol in our stream, it is now assigned the shortest codeword. If the next symbol we read is another B, the output will now be 0 instead of the previous 10.

By dynamically updating the probabilities of symbols as we come across them, we can adjust the sizes of the codewords that are assigned to them, if necessary.

Decoding

Just to ensure that this actually works, let's take a look at the decoding process.

Let's begin again with our setup frequencies[6] and the following VLC table:

Symbol	Probability	Code
A	0.45	0
B	0.45	10
C	0.1	11

We take the next bits of the input stream, see 10, and output B. We also update our probability table, because we've seen another B.

Symbol	Updated probability	Updated code
A	0.4	10
B	0.5	0
C	0.1	11

Lo and behold, the table is evolving in the same way as when we were encoding.

Everything works!

And, as long as our decoder is updating its symbol table in the same fashion as the encoder, the two will always be in synchronization.

Check it out:

Encoding
1. Read symbol from input stream.
2. Output that symbol's codeword to the output stream.
3. Update the symbol table probabilities and regenerate codewords.

Decoding
1. Read the codeword from the input stream.
2. Output that codeword's symbol to the output stream.
3. Update the symbol table probabilities and regenerate codewords.

This is the basic process of how adaptive statistical encoding works. The encoder and decoder are both dynamically updating their probability tables for symbols, which affects the compression, usually in a positive way.

---

6 Note that these starting frequencies are being provided simply as an educational aid. In the real world, you won't get information like this and will have to build your tables from scratch.

Literals

But now we run into two challenges:

- What does our VLC table look like at the start, before we have encoded anything?
- What happens during decoding, when we read in a symbol that doesn't yet exist in our VLC table?

They are actually variations on the same problem, and the answer is: *literal tokens.*

A literal token is a unique "fake" symbol that the encoder and decoder use to signal that it's time to read/write a symbol from the *literal stream*. The literal stream is a second stream that only holds literal values; that is, the actual, encoded symbols in the order in which they are encountered first in the data stream.

For example, for the datastream "AAAAABCABC" the literal stream would be "LIT-ERAL/A/B/C," and the encoded stream might look like **00 1010 01 00 00 00 01 1011 01 1100 00 10 11**, as shown in Figure 6-1.

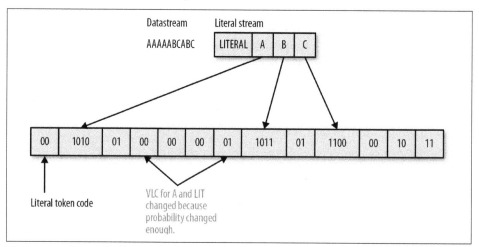

Figure 6-1. Example illustrating how literal tokens, reading from the literal stream, and changed probabilities appear in an encoded data stream.

During encoding, when the encoder reads a symbol it hasn't come across before, it does two things:

1. It emits the LITERAL codeword to the output bit stream.
2. It appends the new symbol to the literal stream.

And during decoding, when the decoder reads a LITERAL codeword, it does these two things:

1. It reads the next literal from the literal stream.

2. It adds that literal to the output and updates its VLC table.

Let's take a look at an example.

When we start encoding our stream, we haven't seen any symbols yet, so we know that for the very first symbol we read, we'll need to emit a literal. It's our only option. As such, we begin our VLC table with LITERAL being the only symbol present, with 100% probability, and a single bit codeword.

Symbol	Probability	Code
<LITERAL>	1.0	00

When we encounter a new symbol from the input stream, we first output the VLC for the LITERAL codeword, followed by the bits for the new symbol. And just like before, we then update our table and probabilities accordingly.

Symbol	Probability	Code
<LITERAL>	0.5	00
A	0.5	01

Suppose that after that we read another A. And then we read B, another new symbol, and having arrived at <LITERAL> A A <LITERAL> B, our probabilities now are:

Symbol	Probability	Code
<LITERAL>	0.4	01
A	0.4	00
B	0.2	10

So, for our input string AAAAABCABC, here is the complete algorithmic example. (You can refer back to Figure 6-1 for visual cues.)

The unencoded 4-bit values for our literals are:

A = 1010

B = 1011

C = 1100

Note that, for our VLC codes, we're just using 00, 01, 10, 11 to keep the explanation simple.

1. Our VLC table contains LITERAL with a 1.0 probability, and its VLC is 00.

2. Read the first symbol, A.

   a. The symbol is not in our table, so we must emit a literal token (which is 00) and then the value of A: 1010.

   b. Add A to our VLC table and update it based upon frequency. Since A and LITERAL have both been seen once, their probability is 0.5 each, and we assign them the codes: LIT=00, A=01.

3. Read the next symbol, A.

   a. Since A is in the table, emit its VLC (01).

   b. Update the table. A is now the most dominant symbol, and thus the VLCs get reassigned: A=00, LIT=01.

4. Read the next symbol, A.

   a. Emit A's VLC (00) and update the probabilities in the table.

5. Read the next symbol, A.

   a. Emit A's VLC (00) and update the table.

6. Read the next symbol, A.

   a. Emit A's VLC (00) and update the table.

7. Read the next symbol, C.

   a. C is not in our table, so emit a literal token (01) and then the value of C, which is 1100.

   b. Add C to our VLC table, and update; A=00, LIT=01, B=10, C=11.

8. Read the next symbol, A.

   a. Emit A's VLC (00) and update the table.

9. Read the next symbol, B.

   a. Emit B's VLC (10) and update the table.

10. Read the next symbol, C.

    a. Emit C's VLC (11) and update the table.

And voilà, the resulting stream is: **00 1010 01 00 00 00 01 1011 01 1100 00 10 11** (see Figure 6-2.)

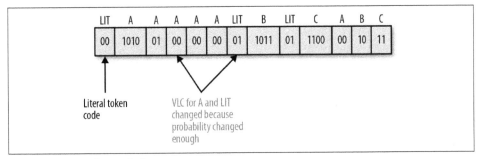

Figure 6-2. Final encoded stream.

Next, can you decode this by reversing the steps?

Resets

The real power of adaptive statistical encoding comes from being able to reset the stream when the output entropy gets out of hand.

Let's take [AAABBBBBCCCCCC] and represent literals as their values in angle brackets, such as <A>.

As we encode this stream, we end up with the following:

<A>,0,0,<B>,1,1,1,0,<C>,11,11,11,11,0

Note that the last 0 for the last C is when the probabilities finally shifted to change the code for C. You can see how with more symbols, and more runs of symbols, the overall bits-per-symbol for output will suffer. It would have been ideal instead to somehow reset our VLC table when we got to C so that we could use 0 for all Cs for a better result and end up with something like this:

<A>,0,0,<B>,1,1,1,0,<C>, <RESET>0,0,0,0,0

As it turns out, we can employ the same tactic that we used with literals and create a <RESET> token, as shown in the example table that follows. Whenever the decoder encounters this token, it resets its symbol table and begins decoding afresh. The encoding and decoding algorithms work the same as before.

The <RESET> and <LITERAL> tokens stay in the symbol table (like any other symbol) and over time, become lower probabilities as they become less frequent.

Following is an example table showing that <RESET> and <LITERAL> tokens will eventually become lower-probability symbols.

Symbol	Probability	Original interval
<LITERAL>	0.05	1110
<RESET>	0.05	1111
A	0.4	00
B	0.3	10
C	0.2	110

Knowing When to Reset

But how do you know when to emit a reset token?

To make the decision to reset, we need to do three things:

- Choose a threshold for resetting; that is, at how many bits-per-symbol (BPS) we are going to pull the plug and start from scratch.
- Measure roughly the average BPS that we have emitted to the output stream so far and compare that to our threshold.
- Calculate the current entropy for the input stream we've read so far.

When the BPS for the output stream exceeds a chosen threshold, say, 5 bits greater than BPS, we can assume that the stream has significantly changed, and we should reset all our statistics.

Specifically, if we track the entropy for the input symbols, we'll find that the number of bits in the output stream will generally be larger than that entropy value. Or, stated formally:

$$Entropy * numSymbolsSoFar > len(outputbits)$$

This is because we can't represent fractional bits in modern hardware. Instead, we can divide the number of output bits by the number of input symbols to give us the "average output BPS," as shown here:

$$aobp = len(outputbits)/numSymbolsSoFar$$

When we compare entropy to aopb, the result shows us how much the output stream is drifting from the estimated desired number of BPS.

When we drift past our threshold (abs(aopb-Entropy) > threshold), we should reset, because the output bitstream is getting *too* bloated.

Threshold isn't a hard-and-fast rule and varies depending on the data stream/encoder. Each encoder that supports this type of reset has fine-tuned these parameters for the particular data it is designed to handle.

Using This in Practice

So, it's worth pointing out that no one uses this simplified version of adaptive VLCs in any real capacity. The same problems with the static version of VLCs follow over to the streaming adaptation. Instead, most modern compressors have jumped entirely to using adaptive versions of Huffman and arithmetic coders that allow for dynamic probability table generation and updated codeword selection.

However, these last few sections were not in vain. The same concepts that power dynamic VLCs—that is, dynamic probability tables, resets, and literals—are all very much present in the adaptive Huffman and adaptive arithmetic coders.

Adaptive Arithmetic Coding

Arithmetic coding is quite easy to make adaptive. This is mostly due to the simplicity of the interaction between the coding step and the probability table. As long as the encoder and decoder agree about how to update the probabilities in the correct order, we can change these tables as we see fit.

Here is a very simple example. Our assumed probability table is as follows, so far:

Symbol	Probability	Original interval
R	0.4	[0, 0.4)
G	0.5	[0.4, 0.9)
B	0.1	[0.9, 1.0)

1. We read in the next input symbol; let's assume that it's the letter G.

2. We encode the symbol using the current probabilities.

3. We update the probability tables with the new information. (We are just going to assume values for the table that follows for this example because we didn't define the preceding stream.)

4. We reassign the intervals.

Symbol	Updated probability	Updated interval
R	0.3	[0.4,0.55)
G	0.6	[0.55, 0.85)
B	0.1	[0.85, 0.9)

And here is how this plays out as a diagram:

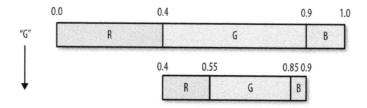

The decoder works in the opposite way. Given the current probability, find the symbol that corresponds to the current numeric output value, update the tables, and reassign the intervals.

Adding literal and reset tokens works in the same way as adaptive VLC. You designate these tokens types as additional symbols, and adjust their weights accordingly.

Adaptive Huffman Coding

Making Huffman coding adaptive isn't as straightforward as it was for arithmetic. This is mainly due to the complexity that arises when dealing with the Huffman tree data structure.

Consider the problem: to properly output a codeword, a full Huffman tree is required. A naive implementation would simply recompute the entire Huffman tree for each symbol that's encountered. This would work, although at the cost of a huge amount of compute performance.

So, rather than rebuilding the entire tree each time, the adaptive Huffman version modifies the existing tree as symbols are being read and processed. Which is where things get a little crazy, because for each symbol read you must do the following:

- Update the probabilities.
- Shuffle and reorder a large number of nodes in the tree to keep them accurate with respect to the changing probabilities.
- Stay compliant with the required structure of the Huffman tree.

The original versions of this adaptive Huffman method were developed in 1973 by Faller,[7] and substantially improved by Knuth in 1985.[8] But modern variants are all

---

7 Newton Faller, "An Adaptive System for Data Compression," in *Record of the 7th Asilomar Conference on Circuits, Systems, and Computers* (IEEE, 1973), 593–597.

8 Donald E. Knuth, "Dynamic Huffman Coding," *Journal of Algorithms*, 6 (1985): 163–180.

built on Vitter's method, introduced in 1987.[9] Refer to the papers referenced in the footnotes, if you'd like to dig into the specifics.

The Modern Choice

These dynamic adaptations have a few benefits over their static counterparts:

- Ability to generate the symbol-to-codeword table rather than storing it explicitly in the stream. This can trade data-stream size for additional compute performance, but more important, this enables the next two benefits.

- Ability to compress data as it arrives, rather than needing to process the set as a whole. This lets you process much larger data sets efficiently, and you don't even need to know ahead of time how large your stream is going to be.

- Ability to adapt to locality of information; that is, adjacency can influence code lengths. This can significantly improve the compression rate.

These three points are very important for modern statistical encoding. As the amount of data is growing, more and more of it is sent over the Internet, and increasingly, people consume data on mobile devices, which have limited storage and stingy data plans. As such, the majority of statistical encoders concern themselves with compressing images (WebP (*https://en.wikipedia.org/wiki/WebP*)) and video (WebM (*https://en.wikipedia.org/wiki/WebM*), H.264 (*http://bit.ly/29H5NHH*)).

What this means for you, however, is that for small data sets, the simplicity of static statistical encoders might work fine, and help you to achieve entropy with very low complexity. If you're working on larger data sets, or multimedia ones for which runtime performance is critical, adopting the adaptive versions is the right choice.

---

9 Jeffrey S. Vitter, "Design and Analysis of Dynamic Huffman Codes," Journal of the ACM, 34: 4 (1987): 825, October.

CHAPTER 7

Dictionary Transforms

Even though information theory was created in the 1940s, Huffman encoding in the 1950s, and the Internet in the 1970s, it wasn't until the 1980s that data compression truly became of practical interest.

As the Internet took off, people began to share images and other data formats that are considerably larger than text. This was during a time when bandwidth and storage were either limited, expensive, or both, and data compression became the key to alleviating these bottlenecks.

With mobile devices on the march to world dominance, we are actually experiencing these same bottlenecks all over again today.

Although variable-length coding (VLC) was churning away at content, the fact that it was locked to entropy produced a limiting gate on the future of compression. So, while the majority of researchers were trying to find more efficient variable-length encodings,[1] a few researchers found new ways for preprocessing a stream to make the statistical compression more impactful.

The result was what's called "dictionary transforms," which completely changed the mentality and value of data compression with respect to the masses. Suddenly, compression became a useful algorithm for all sorts of data types. So useful, in fact, that all of today's dominant compression algorithms (think gzip (*http://www.gzip.org/*

---

[1] Seriously though, Peter Elias had like 30+ VLCs credited to him.

#intro) or 7-Zip (*http://www.7-zip.org*)) use a dictionary transform as their core transformation step. So, let's see what it's all about.

A Basic Dictionary Transform

Statistical compression mostly focuses on a single symbol's probability in a stream, independent of adjacent symbols that might exist around it. This is great for compressing Pi to the *N*th digit, but does not take into account an essential property of real data: context, groupings, or simply put, phrases.

 There are "phrases" in other contexts, too: the rules of music, color composition in images, or the beating of your heart. Basically, any place where there's a grouping of similar content that's available to be repeated later.

For example, rather than encoding each letter of the phrase "TO BE OR NOT TO BE" as a unique symbol, we could, instead, use actual English words as our tokens. The result would create a symbol-to-codeword table that could look something like this (ignoring spaces):[2]

Symbol	Frequency	Codeword
TO	0.33	00
BE	0.33	01
OR	0.16	10
NOT	0.16	11

Which would give us 000110110011 for the encoded string. An original, per-letter encoding would have produced 104 bits, where the word-specific version was compressed to 12 bits.

When we stop considering single symbols, and instead begin considering groups of adjacent symbols,[3] we move out of statistical compression and into the world of *dictionary transforms*.

---

2 If you wonder why this made-up table doesn't add up to 1, it's because of rounding errors. 1/L is 16.66666....

3 Or perhaps more specifically, statistical compressors just accept whatever symbols you throw at them. Dictionary transforms take a given set of symbols and redefine what symbols to use to produce lower entropy for the stream.

Dictionary transforms work much like you'd expect. Given a source stream, first construct some dictionary of words (rather than symbols), and then apply statistical compression based on the words in the dictionary.

Dictionary transforms are not meant to be a replacement for statistical encoding, but rather a transform that you first apply to your stream, so that it can be encoded more effectively by a statistical encoder, as shown in Figure 7-1.

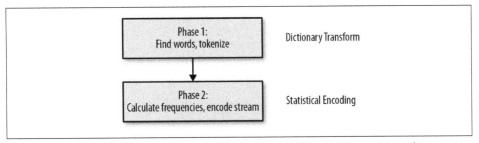

Figure 7-1. Applying a dictionary transform first can produce a data stream that can then be compressed more effectively by statistical encoding.

As such, dictionary transforms represent a preprocessing stage that's applied to a data stream to produce a data set that is smaller and more compressible than the source stream.

A dictionary transform is most effective when it can identify long often-repeated substrings of the data, and assign them the smallest codewords.

Finding the Right "Words"

One big question is, "What represents the best words?" Well, the best words are those that in combination result in the smallest entropy. The bigger question is: How do we determine what those words are?[4]

Our previous example might have been a bit too easy, given that we could split on the spaces in the string and use our very eyes to identify the duplicates.

What about this next string? Looks a bit tougher, maybe?

TOBEORNOTTOBEORTOBEORNOT

Given that there's no simple way to separate words out in this string (without teaching your computer the English language), how do you go about finding them?

---

4 We're using the terms "letter" and "word" here to mean "single symbol" and "multiple adjacent symbols," respectively. To be clear, you can use dictionary transforms on any type of data, not just text.

You do it by using a process known as *tokenization*, which is parsing a set of data to find the ideal "words." Tokenization is so complex that it has its very own branch of research (and associated patents) in the information theory field. For this book, we are going to stick with the basics.

As a baseline, let's first take a look at what our example stream would look like, if we tokenized with single-symbol values—that is, by the letters:

TOBEORNOTTOBEORTOBEORNOT

Token	# occurrence	
O	8	Entropy = 2.38
T	5	
B	3	
E	3	
R	3	
N	2	

Tokenizing by the letters, we end up with an entropy of about 2.38, given that the letters "O" and "T" are duplicated often.

So that's good to know, but let's go the other way. Instead of the smallest symbols, let's tokenize around the longest substring that repeats in the string:

TOBEORNOTTOBEORTOBEORNOT

Token	# occurrence	
TOBEORNOT	2	Entropy = 2.5
O	2	
T	1	
B	1	
E	1	
R	1	

The longest string is "TOBEORNOT", and it is matched twice in the input string. If we assign it a single codeword, the entropy of such a tokenization is about 2.5, which is larger than just using our single-symbol stream, so not a win for our data.

The reason for the increase in entropy is that now there is no clear skewing of the data toward a single dominant symbol. [O,T,B,E,R,TOBEORNOT] are roughly equally probable in this scenario, and thus, are assigned (roughly) the same number of bits.

We could instead parse around the most frequent substrings, which would yield the tokens TOBEOR and NOT. This results in an entropy that's better at 2.2, but not particularly impressive:

TOBEORNOTTOBEORTOBEORNOT

Token	# occurrence
TOBEOR	3
NOT	2

Entropy = 2.2

So, let's try a different approach and tokenize by finding the shortest words with a length greater than 1: TO, BE, OR, NOT and an entropy of 1.98, which is the best we've found for this example:

TOBEORNOTTOBEORTOBEORNOT

Token	# occurrence
TO	3
BE	3
OR	3
NOT	2

Entropy = 1.98

Ah, so we're back to parsing the string based on English words. Although this setup produces the lowest entropy, it's difficult to see how you would properly parse a string to create these optimal sizes.

A brute-force method would read in a group of symbols ("TO") and search the rest of the string to determine its frequency. If the frequency was a good match for the existing symbol table, the algorithm could continue on to the next symbol group and repeat the process. Otherwise, it would try a different group of symbols (such as "TOB"). Sadly though, this would not only require a lot of memory, but take a very long time for any real-life data stream. As such, it's not really suited to any type of real-time processing.

The truth is that to find the ideal tokenization for a stream, we need some way to process symbols we haven't come across before and those that we have, alongside the ability to combine them into the longest symbol sets possible, in some sort of performant manner.

The Lempel-Ziv Algorithm

In 1977, researchers Abraham Lempel and Jacob Ziv invented a few solutions to this "ideal tokenization" problem. The algorithms were named **LZ77** and **LZ78** and are so good at finding optimal tokenization, that in 30+ years, there hasn't been another algorithm to replace them.

Meet Lempel and Ziv

Lempel and Ziv represent a powerhouse duo in the world of data compression.

Jacob Ziv grabbed his undergraduate degrees at the Israeli Institute of Technology (Technion) before earning his doctorate in Information Theory at MIT in 1961. Ziv chose MIT for his doctorate after finding a passion for communications engineering (*http://ethw.org/Oral-History:Jacob_Ziv*), and seeing that Claude Shannon, Peter Elias, and Bob Gallager were all collecting there; basically, he saw the rockstars of information theory all converging at one place, and wanted to be in the center of that research world. After working at Bell Labs for some time, he went back to become a professor at Technion.

Abraham Lempel has a similar story. He fetched his BS, MS, and Doctorate all at the same Technion institute. He then went on to become a professor there, where he met Ziv, and work began on information theory research.

Lempel and Ziv's contributions to the world of information theory have been tremendous and were recognized as such when they received the 1997 Claude E. Shannon Award (*https://en.wikipedia.org/wiki/Claude_E._Shannon_Award*) from the IEEE Information Theory Society (*https://en.wikipedia.org/wiki/IEEE_Informa tion_Theory_Society*).

The LZ77 (*http://bit.ly/29H66SO*)and LZ78 (*http://bit.ly/29H66SO*) algorithms authored by Lempel (*https://en.wikipedia.org/wiki/Abraham_Lempel*) and Jacob Ziv (*https://en.wikipedia.org/wiki/Jacob_Ziv*) have led to a number of derivative works, including the Lempel–Ziv–Welch (*http://bit.ly/29H5X1R*) algorithm, used in the GIF (*https://en.wikipedia.org/wiki/GIF*) image format, and the Lempel–Ziv–Markov chain algorithm (*http://bit.ly/28KCeka*), used in the 7-Zip (*https://en.wikipedia.org/wiki/7-Zip*) and xz (*https://en.wikipedia.org/wiki/Xz*) compressors. The algorithms have also been used as originally published in formats such as DEFLATE (*https://en.wikipe*

---

dia.org/wiki/DEFLATE), which is used in the PNG (*http://bit.ly/29H5JYv*) image format, PKZIP (*https://en.wikipedia.org/wiki/PKZIP*), gzip (*http://www.gzip.org*), and zlib (*http://www.zlib.net*).

For the full interactive story, check out this Compressor Head video (*https://www.youtube.com/watch?v=Jqc418tQDkg*).

How LZ Works

LZ creates a tokenization by trying to match a current word with a previous occurrence of that same word. Rather than reading in a few symbols and then searching ahead to see if there might be duplicates, LZ works by instead looking behind to see if this word has been seen before. This has two main ramifications to the encoding process (see Figure 7-2):

- Earlier in the stream, you'll have seen fewer words, so incoming words will more likely be new. Later in the stream, you'll have a larger buffer to pull from, and matches are more likely.
- Looking backward lets you find the "longest matching word."

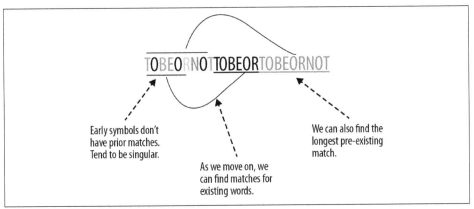

Figure 7-2. The LZ algorithm looks backward to find the longest previously encountered matching word.

The search buffer

The backbone of the LZ algorithm works by splitting the stream into two segments.

- The left side of the stream is dubbed the "search buffer"; it contains the symbols that we've already encountered and processed.

- The right side of the stream is dubbed the "look ahead buffer"; it contains the symbols we're looking to encode.

As such, the current "reading" position in the stream is at the point between the two buffers, as demonstrated in Figure 7-3.

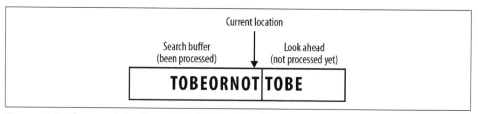

Figure 7-3. The search buffer and look ahead buffer are separated by the current reading location in the stream.

Finding matches

Finding matches is a bit of an organic interplay between the look ahead and search buffers.

Figures 7-4 through 7-9 show how this works.

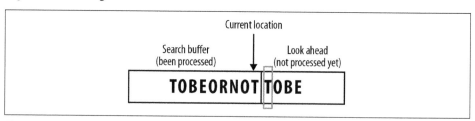

Figure 7-4. From the current location, read one symbol, which is T.

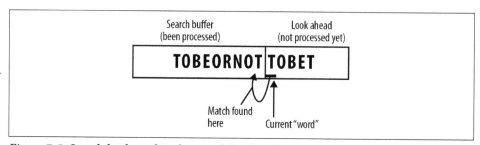

Figure 7-5. Search backward in the search buffer. The first symbol we see is a matching T.

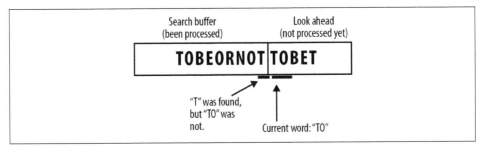

Figure 7-6. Because we are looking for the longest possible match, we now read a second symbol from the look ahead, which is O.

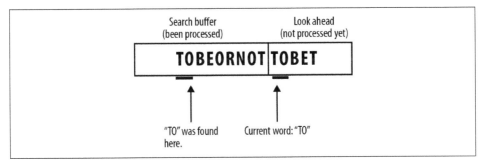

Figure 7-7. There is no O after our matched T in the search buffer, so we go further backward, until eventually we find TO.

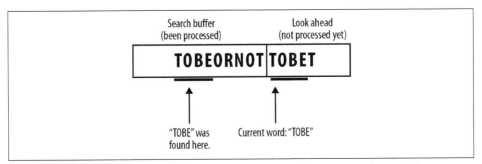

Figure 7-8. We now read the next symbol B, and we still have a match…and the next symbol E, and we are still matching, but looking at the next symbol T, it no longer matches, so we have found the longest match for this sequence of symbols.

Figure 7-9. We encode this match (as described in the next section) and shift the "current position" of the stream to the end of the longest matched word in our look ahead buffer, and ... GOTO 1.

The "sliding window"

Now, in practical implementations, where the stream may be millions of tokens long, we can't look back at the entirety of our already processed stream. Keeping an indefinite search buffer would run into memory and performance problems. As such, the search buffer typically only includes the last 32 KB of processed symbols. So, as we move the current location, we also move a *sliding window* search buffer along our stream, as illustrated in Figure 7-10.

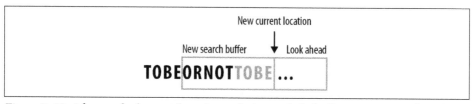

Figure 7-10. After we find a match and encode it, we shift the "current position" to the end of the longest matched word in the look ahead buffer, and the sliding window search buffer moves up to the new current location.

Having a sliding window puts an upper limit on the performance required to find a match. It also makes assumptions about locality, namely that there is a higher chance of correlated data existing at locally similar points in the given data set.

> In general, the sliding window search buffer is some tens-of-thousands of bytes long, whereas the look ahead buffer is only tens of bytes long.

Marking a match with a token

When a match is finally settled on, the encoder will generate a fixed-length token to an output stream. A token is made up of primarily two parts: offset and length.[5]

Offset value
    This represents the position of the start of the matched word in the current search buffer, working backward from the current position. In our example, the matched string was found nine symbols back from the current position mark.

Length value
    This represents the length of the matched word. In our example, the match was four symbols long.

Because for our example we found a match 9 symbols back in the search buffer, with a match-length of 4, the pair [9,4] is emitted to the output as our token, as shown in Figure 7-11.

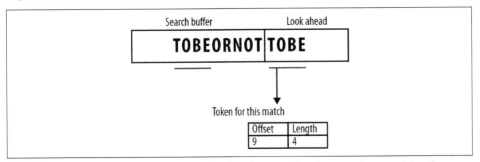

Figure 7-11. Tokens in the look-ahead buffer that match tokens in the search buffer are encoded with their offset from the matching token and their length.

The decoder will un-transform these values in very simple ways:

1. Read the next token

2. From the current position, count offset symbols backward in the search buffer

3. Grab the length number of symbols and append them to the data stream

---

5 It's worth noting that in the original LZ77 and LZ78 papers, the token was a triplet, where the third value was the next symbol in the look-ahead stream, which helped with recovery and processing during decoding. Most modern variants of LZ have done away with the need for this third value, so we generally ignore it in the description.

When no match is found

There are situations for which no match is found in the search buffer for the symbol in the look ahead buffer. In this case, we need to emit some information that lists this new token, so that the decoder can recover it properly.

To do this, we emit a modified token that signifies that our output is a literal value, which the decoder can read and recover to the stream. How this token is constructed is entirely up to the flavor of LZ implementation. As a most basic approach, the algorithm would output a token that has 0 for its offset and 0 for its length [0,0], followed by the literal symbol, as shown in Figure 7-12.

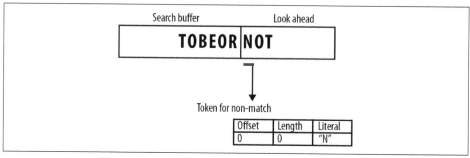

Figure 7-12. Tokens for nonmatched symbols are unique and typically include the literal symbol for the decoder to read.

Encoding

Given our input stream "TOBEORNOTTOBE", let's walk through an example encoding (see also the table that follows).

1. The first four symbols have no match in the search buffer, and are easily output to literal tokens.

2. When we get to the second letter "O" in the look ahead, we find a single matching symbol in the search buffer, giving us a token of (3,1).

3. This process continues on for a while, finding either nonmatches or single-value matches.

4. Where things get interesting, is when we get to the end of the string, and see TOBE matched, back at the beginning of the search buffer, at location 9 and with a length of 4.

Search buffer	Look ahead buffer	Output
	TOBEORNOTTOBE	0,0,T
T	OBEORNOTTOBE	0,0,O
TO	BEORNOTTOBE	0,0,B
TOB	EORNOTTOBE	0,0,E
TOBE	ORNOTTOBE	3,1
TOBEO	RNOTTOBE	0,0,R
TOBEOR	NOTTOBE	0,0,N
TOBEORN	OTTOBE	3,1
TOBEORNO	TTOBE	8,1
TOBEORNOT	TOBE	9,4
		\<eos\>

Decoding

The decoding process works off of the tokens:

- When the decoder finds a literal token, it emits the value directly to the search buffer.
- If it finds a "match" token, it will count from the current position to the offset and append the number of characters indicated by the length to the end of the recovered buffer.

Input token	Recovered buffer
0,0,T	
0,0,O	T
0,0,B	TO
0,0,E	TOB
3,1	TOBE
0,0,R	TOBEO
0,0,N	TOBEOR
3,1	TOBEORN
8,1	TOBEORNO
9,4	TOBEORNOT
\<eos\>	

There you go, pretty straightforward, eh?

Compressing LZ output

It's pretty easy to see that the LZ transform produces (in most cases) a smaller encoded form of the data stream than the source form. (We think that any opportunity to
replace a 12-symbol word with a 2-symbol token is a win in our book.[6]) That's the
main draw here, that for streams with lots of duplicate words, you can encode them
in much smaller sets of tokens.

However, what makes LZ truly attractive is that you can combine it with a statistical
encoder. You do this by separating the offset, length, and literal values from the
tokens into their own contiguous sets, and then apply a statistical compressor to each
of them.

For example, you can separate our example token set [0,0,T][0,0,O][0,0,B][0,0,E][3,1]
[0,0,R][0,0,N][3,1][8,1][9,4] into these three data sets:

Offsets 0,0,0,0,3,0,0,3,8,9
Lengths 0,0,0,0,1,0,0,1,1,4
Literals T,O,B,E,R,N

Now, each of these streams has different properties and can be approached differently.

Offsets

Firstly, we know that offsets will always be in the range of $[0,X]$, where X is the length
of the search buffer. So in the worst case, offsets are encoded with $\log_2(X)$ bits per
value, allowing you to index any byte in the sliding window.

Sadly, offsets tend to be all over the place, so there's not a lot of duplicated content in
large streams. However, applying a statistical encoder could still yield good results.
For example, the offsets listed in our stream have an entropy of 1.57, but expect that
to get worse as your data set gets larger. A worst case scenario here is a match at every
location in your buffer, which produces every unique, nonduplicated value in this
stream.

Lengths

Lengths have a similar problem. They can generally be any size, so our only hope to
compress this data further is to take advantage of duplicate symbols by using a statistical encoder. This value set tends to skew itself toward duplicates around the type of
language and input you're using. For example, if you're encoding a book written in

---

6 As the authors, this *is* our book, so yeah...wins all around.

English, there will be lots of length 2, 3, and 4 tokens in your set. For our previous example, the lengths set has an entropy of 1.30, which would give us ~13 bits to encode the length data.

Literals

For our small example, literals don't seem to have any better compression than the offsets and lengths. However, as the size of the input stream grows, the entropy of the literal stream drops slightly, as duplicate literal values might exist (because of the sliding window). Whether this can happen also depends on the size of the search buffer. For example, if you have two B tokens that are separated by exactly 32,000 other tokens, they may be too far apart to create a valid match. As such, the literal stream would have two B symbols in it.

LZ Variants

The LZ algorithm is excessively powerful, but equally impressive is how many variants of the algorithm have been created over the past 40 years (see Figure 7-13). Each one tweaks the basic LZ77 just slightly, depending on the specific need, performance, or use case. We'll cover a few of the important ones here and let you search for the rest on your own.

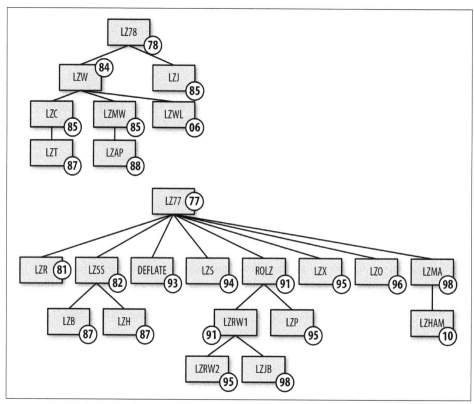

Figure 7-13. A lineage of the LZ77 and LZ78 algorithms that shows the variants and the years they were created.

LZ77

The basic LZ77 algorithm (sometimes called LZ1) works much like what we've described previously; however, each token will always output, as its third value, the literal of the next character in the look-ahead buffer.

LZSS

The main difference between LZ77 and LZSS is that in LZ77 the dictionary reference could actually be longer than the string it is replacing. In LZSS, such references are omitted, if the length of the string is less than the "break even" point. Furthermore, LZSS uses one-bit flags to indicate whether the next chunk of data is a literal (byte) or a reference to an offset-length pair.

Many popular archivers like PKZip (*https://en.wikipedia.org/wiki/PKZip*), ARJ (*https://en.wikipedia.org/wiki/ARJ*), RAR (*http://bit.ly/29H64dK*), ZOO (*http://bit.ly/29H69y1*), and LHarc (*http://bit.ly/29H6pgB*) used LZSS as their primary compression algorithm. And as a nostalgia moment: The Game Boy Advance (*http://bit.ly/ 29H6j8L*) BIOS had built-in functionality to decode a modified LZSS format for patching and so on.

LZ78 or LZ2

The core LZ algorithms published back in 1977 and 1978 are sometimes called LZ1 and LZ2. LZ78 works mostly as we've just described, but rather than using an offset to the search buffer, LZ78 will create references to a dictionary that is built based on the input stream.

LZW (Lempel–Ziv–Welch)

LZW was published in 1984 by Terry Welch (*https://en.wikipedia.org/wiki/ Terry_Welch*) and builds on the idea of the LZ78 algorithm. Here's how it works:

1. LZW initializes a dictionary with all the possible input characters, as well as clear and stop codes, if they're used.

2. The algorithm scans through the input string for successively longer substrings until it finds one that is not in the dictionary.

3. When such a string is found, the index for the string without the last character (i.e., the longest substring that is in the dictionary) is retrieved from the dictionary and sent to output.

4. The new string (now including the last character) is added to the dictionary.

5. And the same last input character is then used as the starting point to scan for the next substring.

In this way, successively longer strings are registered in the dictionary and made available for subsequent encoding as single output values. The algorithm works best on data with repeated patterns, because the initial parts of a message will see little compression. As the message grows, however, the compression ratio tends asymptotically to the maximum.

LZW compression became the first widely used universal data compression method on computers. LZW was used in the public-domain program "compress" (*https:// en.wikipedia.org/wiki/Compress*), which became a more or less standard utility in Unix systems circa 1986. It has since disappeared from many distributions, both because it infringed the LZW patent and because gzip produced better compression ratios using the LZ77-based DEFLATE algorithm.

Collect Them All!

The point being that, again, there's a huge number of potential input data sets, and each one responds to each algorithm in a specific way. Knowing your data set can help you pick the best LZ transform for it.

CHAPTER 8

Contextual Data Transforms

Before we begin with this chapter, let's take a moment to recap.

Statistical encoders work by assigning a variable-length codeword to a symbol. Compression comes from smaller codewords being given to more frequently occurring symbols. The tokenization process of dictionary transforms works by identifying the longest, most probable symbols for a data set. Effectively, they find the best symbols for a set so that it can be encoded more efficiently. Technically speaking, we could just use the process to identify the best symbols and then plug that back into a statistical encoder to get some compression. However, the real power of the LZ method is that we don't do that; instead, we represent matching information as a series of output pairs with lower entropy, which we then compress.

In addition to dictionary transforms, there's an entire suite of other great transforms that work on the same principle: given some set of adjacent symbols, transform them in a way that makes them more compressible. We like to call these kinds of transforms "contextual," because they all take into account preceding or adjacent symbols when considering ideal ways to encode the data.

The goal is always to transform the information in such a way that statistical encoders can come through and compress the results in a more efficient manner.

You could transform your data in lots of different ways, but there are three big ones that matter the most to modern data compression: *run-length encoding*, *delta coding*, and *Burrows–Wheeler transform*.

Let's pick them apart.

Run-Length Encoding

Run-length encoding (RLE) is one of the most deceptively simple and powerful encoding techniques for various data types over the past 40+ years. RLE takes advantage of the adjacent clustering of symbols that occur in succession. It replaces a "run" of symbols with a tuple that contains the symbol and the number of times it is repeated. For example, as Figure 8-1 demonstrates, AAAABBBBBBBBCCCCCCCC is encoded as [A,4][B,8][C,8].[1]

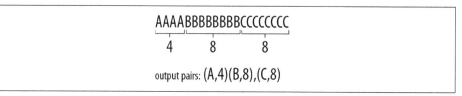

Figure 8-1. RLE identifies runs of identical symbols in a stream. It then transforms the stream into a set of pairs containing the symbol and the length of its run.

From a conceptual level, that's really it. Nothing special after that. Encoding means finding a symbol and scanning ahead to see how long the run is.

Decoding works in the inverse. Given a pair containing the symbol and the length, simply append the proper number of symbols to the output stream.

Dealing with Short Runs

However, not all data is as uniform as our first example. Following the simplistic algorithm, AAAABCCCC would be encoded as [A,4][B,1][C,4]. Because the single B in the middle of the run was expanded from one symbol to a symbol-and-length pair, we have just created bloat in the data stream, as illustrated in Figure 8-2.

---

1 According to "every CS class ever made" and Wikipedia, RLE encoding is typically introduced not as a pairwise transform, but instead would inline the length with symbol values, giving A4B1C4. Truth is, though, that no one actually uses RLE in this form due to the interweaving of literal symbols and numeric values; so it's a complete waste of time to introduce it that way. In fact, we are somewhat sad to have distracted you enough with this footnote by it—sorry about that.

Figure 8-2. Small runs represent large problems for RLE as an algorithm. The overhead of storing short runs impacts the compression size significantly. Take this example, where the many nonduplicated symbols bloat the output.

Now if you're lucky, across your entire stream the amount of overhead from these single symbols will easily be covered by the savings from long runs.

For all other situations, you need a way of identifying runs of characters that are worse off being encoded with RLE, and perhaps should be left alone in the stream, instead. For example, you could encode only runs with two or more symbols.

With that premise, AAAABCCCC would be encoded as [A,4] B [C,4]. Thus, if many characters are not repeated, you will rarely use an unnecessary counter. The problem with this method is that decoding is properly ambiguous. If we translate the transformed stream into binary, we could end up with 100000110010000101000011100,[2] and no real way of distinguishing where the B run ends and the C run begins. Basically, the literal values being interwoven into the data stream is problematic.[3]

As such, we need a way to denote what runs have pairs and what runs don't. A common solution to this is to add to the data set a second bit stream that denotes whether a given stream is long or repeated (Figure 8-3). Thus, the stream of 100000110010000101000011100 would be prepended by a bit stream of 101, denoting that the first symbol is a run, the second is not, and the third is. This helps save you the overhead of small-run streams by instead deferring a single bit-per-run.

---

2 If your eyes just glazed over, that's 7 bits of ASCII per literal, so 1000001|100|1000010|1000011|100.

3 This is a problem we've already had to tackle in this book for adaptive statistical encodings and dictionary transforms: interleaving the literal values in the numeric stream is just asking for trouble.

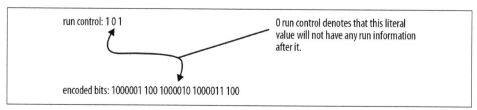

run control: 1 0 1

0 run control denotes that this literal value will not have any run information after it.

encoded bits: 1000001 100 1000010 1000011 100

Figure 8-3. By combining a bit stream denoting which literals are runs, we can properly decode the stream. In this example, the second literal has a 0 for run control, so we don't attempt to read the 3 bit code afterward, which would denote how long the run is.

Important

RLE works best on data sets with looooooooong runs of similar symbols. If your data set does not exhibit those characteristics, RLE won't work for you, and you might want to keep reading and learn about MTF or delta coding, instead.

Compressing

Compressing an RLE'd stream is a bit of a trick. First, split your data set into two sets: a literal stream, and a run-length stream. (Remember the bit stream you prepended? It will tell you from which stream to read during decoding.) You can encode the literal stream by using an encoder of your choice.[4] The run-length stream is really where the compression problems lie. So, using the very real-world method of trial and error, let's find a suitable encoding for it.[5]

Given the lengths [4,3,1,1,1,3,1,2,1,2,1], we could encode them with binary 2 bits per value, giving us 22 bits total. However, this falls over if we get one run of long length, such as [256,3,1,1,1,3,1,2,1,2,1]. In this case, we'd need to encode all the values with the same number of bits as the largest value in the set. So in this case, we'd need to encode every value with 8 bits, making the set 88 bits total. Not ideal.

So, let's move from that to static VLCs. In a naive model, we could assign a run-length integer with the number of bits from the representing VLC. So, if we had the lengths [4,3,1,1,1,3,1,2,1,2,1], we could end up with a *unary encoding* of [11110,1110,10,10,10,1110,10,110,10,110,10], or 31 bits. As you can see, this method fails directly. It assigns the smallest value to the smallest codeword (assuming that it appears most often in the data). RLE lengths are opposite, however, and we want to assign the *largest* values (representing the longest runs) with the smallest codewords.

---

4 LZ is fun to apply, because now you get to look at how often runs of symbols can be duplicated.

5 Even compressors that have multiple algorithms in their arsenal might choose in this manner.

Applying a statistical encoder (such as Huffman or arithmetic compression) might be better. We can get a sense of the impact of those values on our data set by calculating the set's entropy, which is 1.69, giving us an encoded size of ~19 bits (about 13% savings). We could find a lower entropy by applying an adaptive version of a statistical encoder, which might take into account locality, if there is any.

Nerds on the Loose

RLE was originally introduced in a 1966 paper in which Solomon W. Golomb[6] first described his now-famous *Golomb codes* using a novel and informative James Bond–style metaphor:

> Secret Agent 00111 is back at the casino again, playing a game of chance, while the fate of mankind hangs in the balance.

The peer-reviewed and cornerstone paper then went on to describe the probability of symbol occurrences with a metaphor for playing a roulette table, even including a nod to the bartender's influence on the whole thing. This is one of the great examples of true, interesting people inside the world of compression. It's so easy to focus on the algorithms for this type of science that we forget the people who are involved. But the truth is, they were all nerds. Math nerds mostly, but still, silly, quirky nerds who loved numbers and found humorous ways to talk about complex problems.

RLE is considered a single-context model, in that any given symbol considers the previous symbol during encoding. If it's the same, you continue on with the run, and if it's different, you terminate the current run. Even though it's not used often for modern compressors, more efficient RLE methods continue to be researched. For example, a new RLE compressor, TurboRLE (*https://github.com/powturbo/TurboRLE*), has been published recently, and it claims to be the fastest, most efficient RLE encoder of all time.

It's sometimes helpful to think of RLE lengths as a form of delta-encoded values. If you imagined noting the beginning of each run in absolute value, the lengths represent the distance (in symbols) between changes in symbol in the stream.

---

6 S. W. Golomb, "Run-length encodings" (*https://urchin.earth.li/~twic/Golombs_Original_Paper/*), *IEEE Trans. Information Theory*, vol. IT-12, pp. 399–401, July 1966.

Delta Coding

We touched on delta coding a bit earlier, but it's time to go into some deeper details. Numeric data must be some of the most annoying types of data to compress. This is because most of the time, there's no statistical information to exploit. And you run into numerical data everywhere. Think GPS coordinates, inverted indexes from a search engine, and returning user IDs. Consider this lovely block of awesome as an example:

[51, 12, 8, 321, 0, 0, 12, 18, 9, 255, 0, 18, 64]

From an entropy perspective, there's not a lot to work with here. Only a few values are duplicated, and the rest tend to have a high entropy value. In general, we'd need to store this data set in its full 8 bits per value. Thankfully, there's a way to transform this data into a different set of numbers that might have better entropy.

Delta coding is the process of storing a data stream as the relative differences (deltas) between subsequent (i.e., adjacent) values. The idea is that, given a set of data, correlated or similar data tends to cluster around itself. If so, determining the difference between two adjacent values might be able to define one value as the difference from the other. Basically, you subtract the current value from the previous value and store that difference to your output stream.

Delta coding is one of the most important algorithms in modern computing. Given the fact that numeric data is so prevalent in our systems and its entropy is so high, delta coding offers a transform that's not based on statistics; rather, it's based on adjacency. It's most helpful in time-series data (such as a sensor checking the differences in temperature once every 10 seconds), or in media, like audio and images, where locally there's temporal correlation between data.

Take this set of numbers:

[1,3,6,8,10]

Perform the subtractions → and receive this delta-encoded set:

[1,3–1,6–3,8–6,10–8] → [1,2,3,2,2]

The source data roughly needed to be stored using 4 bits each (because $\log_2(10) = 4$). After delta coding, the resulting stream requires only 2 bits per symbol. The result? 10 bits instead of 20.

You can reconstruct the original stream by reversing the process. Adding the previous value to the current offset.

Start with the encoded set:

[1,2,3,2,2]

Perform the additions → and receive this original set:

[1,1+2,3+3,6+2,8+2] → [1,3,6,8,10]

In general, the goal of delta coding is to reduce the dynamic range of the data set. That is, reduce the number of bits needed to represent every value in the data. Which means that Delta coding is most effective when the differences between subsequent values are relatively small. If the differences between values become large, things break down.

Observe this set:

[1,2,10,256]

Perform delta coding → and receive this:

[1,2–1,10–2,256–10] → [1,1,8,246]

Applying delta coding here didn't produce a less dynamic range, and we still need to encode the entire set with $\log_2$(maxValue).

But things could become even worse than that. Consider this sequence of woe:

[1,3,10,8,6]

Perform Delta coding → and cry:

[1,3–1,10–3,8–10,6–8] → [1,2,7,–2,–2]

In this set, we have subsequent values that are larger than their predecessors, and we end up with negative values in the transformed set. The largest positive value is 7, so we could store the positive values as LOG2(7) = 3 bits each. Sadly though, we now need to represent those negative values, meaning that we need to store an extra bit per symbol, requiring 4 bits.

These kinds of situations are extremely common and are exactly where delta coding falls over and becomes less effective. But there's a whole slew of modifications you can apply to make this algorithm more robust, regardless of the data to which you're applying it.

Let's take a look at a few simple examples.

XOR Delta Coding

The issue with subtractive delta coding is that you can end up with negative values, which causes all sorts of problems. Negative values require you to store an extra lead bit, and they also increase the dynamic range of your data, like so:

$$[1,3,10,8,6] \rightarrow [1,3-1,10-3,8-10,6-8] \rightarrow [1,2,7,-2,-2]$$

We can improve this result by replacing subtractions with bitwise exclusive OR (XOR) operations (*https://en.wikipedia.org/wiki/Bitwise_operation#XOR*).

Bitwise Exclusive OR (XOR) Operations

Bitwise operates on each bit independently. Exclusive OR (XOR (*https://en.wikipedia.org/wiki/Bitwise_operation#XOR*)) is a logical operation (*https://en.wikipedia.org/wiki/Logical_connective*) that outputs TRUE only when both inputs differ (one is TRUE, the other is FALSE).

Example:

```
      0101 (decimal 5)
  XOR 0011 (decimal 3)
    = 0110 (decimal 6)
```

Note that you can use XORing with bit strings of 1 to flip bits.

```
      0101 (decimal 5)
  XOR 1111 (decimal 15)
    = 1010 (decimal 10)
```

Also note that XORing any value with itself always yields 0.

In times long gone, when registers were flipped and cleared manually, this was indeed essential knowledge.

XORing bypasses the issue of negatives entirely, because XORing integers never generates negative values.

Starting with: [1,3,10,8,6]

XOR Delta encoded =

$1 \oplus 1 = 0$

$3 \oplus 1 = 11 \oplus 01 = 10 = 2$

$10 \oplus 3 = 1010 \oplus 0011 = 1001 = 9$

$8 \oplus 10 = 1000 \oplus 1010 = 0010 = 2$

$6 \oplus 8 = 0110 \oplus 1000 = 1110 = 14$

Yields: [1,2,9,2,14]

So, this didn't quite reduce the dynamic range, because we still need 4 bits per value, but it *did* keep all our values positive, regardless of the relative ordering of the data.

Frame of Reference Delta Coding

Consider the following sequence:

[107,108,110,115,120,125,132,132,131,135]

We could store these 10 numbers as 8-bit integers using 80 bits in total. But that seems a waste because all those numbers below 107 are just padding space. We're including bits to potentially represent them, but our data set does not include any of those values.

The frame-of-reference approach addresses this problem by subtracting the smallest value from the rest of the numbers. In the example, the numbers range from 107 to 135. Thus, instead of coding the original sequence, we can subtract 107 from each value and delta encode this difference:

[0,1,3,8,13,18,25,25,24,28]

As a result, we can code each offset value using no more than 5 bits.

Of course, we still need to store the minimum value 107 using 8 bits, and we need at least 3 bits to record the fact that only 5 bits per value are used. Nevertheless, the total $8 + 3 + 9 * 5 = 45$ is much less than the original 80 bits.

The "frame" part of "frame of reference" (also called "FOR") has to do with the fact that to apply this transform to your data set properly, you need to subdivide it into smaller blocks (or frames) of numbers.

For instance, we could split our previous set of numbers into these two sets:

[107,108,110,115,120] [125,132,132,131,135]

We'd end up with the following:

[107,0,1,3,8,13] [125,0,7,7,6,10]

And framing our data has helped produce smaller dynamic ranges, and thus it requires fewer bits per value to represent.[7]

Sadly, outliers can still cause problems.

What's This "Frame" Thing?

FOR was originally designed to fit as many numerical values into a single integer space as possible (typically a 32-bit or 128-bit integer). This is ideal for a couple of reasons:

- It makes the values easier to handle with runtime code (because computers prefer word-aligned, power-of-two numeric values), and it also acts as a nifty in-memory compressed representation of things.

- It provides a pretty straightforward compression method. Packing 10 integers into a 32-bit space gives pretty good compression. The result is a massively performant method for decoding billions of integer values in a second at the cost of some additional overhead for integers that don't have a bit space that's fully utilized.

Patched Frame of Reference Delta Coding

Consider the following number set:[8]

[1,2,10,256]

Delta encoded =

[1,2–1,10–2,256–10] = [1, 1, 8, 246]

That outlier is basically breaking compression for the rest of the data.

---

7 The elephant in the room is, of course, how to determine the optimal frame. So far, most implementations have used 32-bit to 128-bit windows, because…well, that fits into a single integer.

8 We know, you've already considered it once in this chapter. So this time, consider it *harder*.

To alleviate this problem, Zukowski et al.[9] proposed a method of patching that they called PFOR.[10]

It works like this:

1. Choose a bit width b.
2. Walk through the data and encode numbers with b bits.
3. When you come to a number that requires more than b bits to encode, store this exception in a separate location.

The exceptions part of PFOR is where the magic comes in.

1. Consider our delta encoded example [1,1,8,246].
2. In a simplistic form, we could split the data into two sets, those values that require b bits and those that don't. With $b = 4$ bits, we'd then get [1,1,8][246].
3. We can now encode the first set with 4 bits, and then the exception in 8 bits.
4. To know where the exceptions get merged back into the source list, we also need a position value, giving us [1,1,8][246][3].

During the decoding phase, we take the exception values and insert them back into the source stream before undoing the delta decoding.

Of course, there are two main questions at this point:

- How do we find the value b?
- What do we do with the exceptions?

Finding b

The goal is to determine the proper bit width b that encodes the most numbers in our set and lets us identify outliers.

You can generally do this incrementally. Begin with 1 bit, test how many values in your set are less than 2^1. If 90% of your data is less than this value, set $b = 1$. Otherwise, increment b to 2, test for $< 2^2$. If necessary, repeat with $b = 3$ and 2^3, and continue until you find the b that works for 90% of your data set.

---

9 M. Zukowski, S. Heman, N. Nes, and P. Boncz, "Super-Scalar RAM-CPU Cache Compression," *Proceedings of the 22nd International Conference on Data Engineering, ICDE '06*, IEEE Computer Society: Washington, DC, USA, 2006; 59–71, doi:10.1109/ICDE.2006.150

10 It's worth noting that PFOR could, technically be applied to a data set independent of Delta coding, which is why you see this algorithm sometimes written as PFD, PFor or PForDelta when used in conjunction with delta coding. Which is how we like to use it, and why it's in this section—it's good to be the authors.

What do we do with exceptions?

One of the interesting problems with PFOR is that, along with your modified delta information, you now end up with a second data set that represents exception data. This second set can have a large dynamic range, and can be difficult to directly compress. According to the original papers (*http://oai.cwi.nl/oai/asset/15564/15564B.pdf*), rather than just throwing the entire exception list into a new list, raw, PFOR can instead leave the lowest "b" bits in the source stream, and store the difference in the exception list.

For example, in the following list, the upper three most-significant bits are zeros, except in one number.

101**0010**

0001**010**

0001**100**

0001**011**

Now, rather than storing an exception set of 101,000,000,000, we can just note that the first location is the only exception we need to care about. The result, is that we now get three new sets.

The first set is the lowest 4 bits of our data:

[0010,1010,1100,1011]

Followed by an index to which values have an exception:

[0]

Followed by the actual exception bits, for those locations:

[101]

The result is that the exception array has a much lower dynamic range and can then be compressed a little better, potentially.

Compressing Delta-Encoded Data

Note that at this point, we haven't actually compressed anything; we've merely transformed the data in such a way that things can potentially be more compressible.[11]

Delta coding produces a more compressible data set when it can do the following:

- Reduce the maximum value in the stream, reducing the dynamic range.
- Produce lots of duplicate values, which allows for more effective statistical compression.

The second is most likely more important because it fits in better with common statistical compression systems. However, if the results of delta coding don't produce statistically variant data, you end up needing to take advantage of the first, which basically moves toward trying to reduce the overall LOG2 for the entire data set.

In general, taking the produced data and then throwing it at any statistical encoder should produce good compression.

Does It Work on Text?

Not really. I mean, it can work, but given that English text oscillates between early sections of the alphabet and later sections of the alphabet, you end up with a lot of positive-negative switches in the data. Plus, other systems like LZ are going to do a ton better.

Move-to-Front Coding

Contextual data transforms operate on the basic philosophy that the linearity of the data (that is, its order) contains some information that helps us encode future symbols. Move-to-front (MTF) is such an encoding. But rather than considering immediate adjacency, like RLE and dictionary encoders do, MTF is more concerned with the general occurrence of a symbol over short windows of data.

The MTF step reflects the expectation that after a symbol has been read from the input stream, it will be read many more times, and will, at least for a while, be a common symbol. The MTF method is locally adaptive because it adapts itself to the frequencies of symbols in local areas of the input stream. The method produces good results if the input stream satisfies this expectation; that is, if it contains concentra-

---

11 In fact, if you reread the previous sections, you'll note that we were very clear to call this technique "delta coding" instead of "delta compression," because technically speaking, the latter is incorrect; there's no compression going on.

tions of identical symbols (if the local frequency of symbols changes significantly from area to area in the input stream).

Figure 8-4 shows that the entire process works by keeping a second array of data, which contains the unique values that exist in the data set. Let's call this the SortedArray. As a value is read from the input stream, we find its location in the SortedArray and output that index to the output stream. Then, we update the SortedArray by moving that value to the *front* of the array, giving it an index of 0.

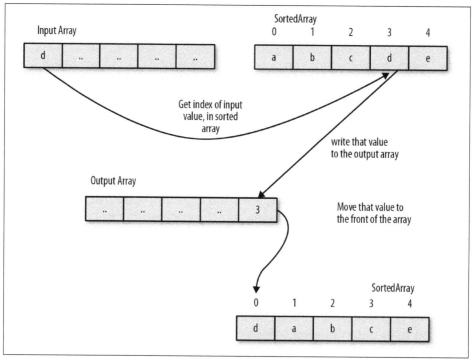

Figure 8-4. A general diagram detailing how MTF works. As a value is met in the input stream multiple times, it will move toward the front of the SortedArray, resulting in lower values being emitted to the output stream.

Here's a simple example. Assume for simplicity's sake that the symbols in the data are lowercase ASCII characters, that our input stream is "banana", and that the symbols in our initial SortedArray are in alphabetical order:

1. Read the letter "b."

2. "b" is at index 1[12] in SortedArray, so we output 1 to the output stream.

---

12 For nonprogrammers: array indices start at 0, so the second position in SortedArray is 1.

3. Move "b" to the front of SortedArray.

4. Read the letter "a," which is now at index 1, output 1, and move "a" back to the front.

5. Continue with the remaining letters, moving through the table.

Input symbol	Output stream	Re-SortedArray
		abcdefghijklmnopqrstuvwxyz
b	1	bacdefghijklmnopqrstuvwxyz
a	1,1	abcdefghijklmnopqrstuvwxyz
n	1,1,14	nabcdefghijklmopqrstuvwxyz
a	1,1,14,1	anbcdefghijklmopqrstuvwxyz
n	1,1,14,1,1	nabcdefghijklmopqrstuvwxyz
a	1,1,14,1,1,1	anbcdefghijklmopqrstuvwxyz

The final output stream is 1,1,14,1,1,1, which has an entropy of 0.65,[13] as opposed to the source stream entropy of 1.46.

The decoder can recover this stream by reversing the process. Given [1,1,14,1,1,1], it starts with a SortedArray of [a,b,...z]. For each symbol the decoder reads from the input stream, it outputs the value at that index in the SortedArray, and then moves that symbol to the front of the SortedArray.

Avoiding Rogue Symbols

One of the issues with MTF is that a few rogue symbols can interrupt a nice stream of symbols that exist at the front. This is one of the more detrimental issues because it can seriously mess up your encoding, and in truth, it's quite common in real-life data.

One solution to this is to not let symbols go to the very front of the list as soon as they are matched; instead, you need to employ some heuristic that slowly moves them to the front. The following example demonstrates how heuristics work quite well in practice.

Move-ahead-k

In this variant, the element of SortedArray that matches the current symbol is moved k positions toward the front, instead of all the way.

You need to figure out the optimal value for k; however, there are two easy choices:

---

13 This really should give Shannon a headache. This is the lowest entropy we have seen in this book, so far.

- Setting $k = n$ (the number of symbols) is identical to the original MTF.
- Setting $k = 1$ allows symbols to move to the front only one step at a time.

Setting $k = 1$ tends to reduce performance for inputs that have local concentrations of symbols, but works better for other inputs. Implementing the algorithm with $k = 1$ is especially simple because updating SortedArray only requires swapping an element with the one preceding it. This variant deals somewhat better with rogue symbols because they must slowly work their way to the front of the stream, rather than going there immediately.

Wait-c-and-move

In this variant, an element of SortedArray is moved to the front only after it has been matched c times to symbols from the input stream (not necessarily consecutive times). Each element of SortedArray has a counter associated with it to count the number of matches. This makes it possible for you to consider a threshold of occurrence before a symbol can approach the front of the stream. When used on text, this will tend to produce a SortedArray that mirrors the commonness of the letters in the language you're encoding.

Compressing MTF

MTF creates a stream of symbols that is expected to have a lower entropy than the source stream. This makes its output a prime candidate to pass off to a statistical compressor for further compression. Because MTF should produce a stream with more 0s and 1s, a simple statistical encoder would work fine.

MTF is unique in that it reassigns a shorter value to symbols as they recur within a short time. RLE, on the other hand, assigns the shortest codes to symbols that occur in clusters. In practice, MTF is one of the simplest forms of dynamic statistical transforms.

Burrows–Wheeler Transform

Every family has a black sheep. Burrows–Wheeler transform (BWT) is one of them. You see, all of the other compression algorithms can generally be categorized as statistical compressors (i.e., VLCs) or dictionary compressors (such as LZ78), which in different ways exploit the statistical redundancies present in a given data stream.

BWT does not work this way. Instead, it works by shuffling the data stream to cluster symbols together. This does not provide compression in and of itself, but it lets you hand off the transformed stream to other compression systems.

How BWT Came to Be

As far as compression algorithms go, BWT must have one of the most interesting genesis stories of the lot.

Back around 1978, David Wheeler stumbled across the first iteration of this transform while visiting Bell Labs. However, at the time, he didn't think much of it. His original vision for the transform was to use it as a benchmark against which to compare other algorithms, because he deemed it too slow to use in practice. In addition, Wheeler's work at the Computer Lab in Cambridge didn't have an aggressive publication requirement, so the algorithm mostly went undiscovered and unreported for the better part of a decade.

Mike Burrows was taught this algorithm by Wheeler while he was a graduate student at the Computer Lab in Cambridge. Burrows just assumed that this was another crazy algorithm you learned while writing your thesis. When Burrows asked Wheeler how he had created the algorithm, he couldn't really remember. There had been some research related to grouping values based on their context, but how the realization was made that the transform was invertible, was never revealed.

It wasn't until years later that Burrows recognized the importance and significance of what the transform did, along with the realization that unless he wrote up the algorithm, it might never be published. So, in 1994, Burrows began working with Wheeler to create a performant implementation, taking advantage of new techniques and the latest computer hardware.

Colt had the pleasure of meeting Dr. Burrows while filming Episode 4 of Compressor Head (*https://www.youtube.com/watch?v=4WRANhDiSHM*), a YouTube series about compression algorithms, and he told him how the original algorithm was published.

"There's a funny story about that. We first sent the paper to the annual Data Compression Conference (*http://www.cs.brandeis.edu/~dcc/*), but they rejected it. There were no comments as to why. And when I asked, they said that it was their policy not to explain why they rejected papers. So, we just published it as a technical report. The algorithm became more well known when someone saw the technical report and published an article about it in Dr. Dobbs Journal. The next year, the people at the same conference asked me to submit the paper again, so that they could publish it. And I said, 'No, and I'm not going to explain why, because it's my policy not to explain that sort of thing.'"

Can you imagine that? Had Burrows never taken the effort to make this algorithm publishable, it might never have seen the light of day. More proof that the world of compression is crazy, a little weird, and certainly holds a grudge.

Ordering Is Important!

One of the issues with entropy as a unit of measure is that it fails to take into account the order of the symbols. Regardless of how we shuffle [1234567890], it always has an entropy of 4.

But we know that order does, in fact, matter greatly. For example, the LZ family of dictionary compressors takes ordering very seriously, as do the other contextual transforms we've shown in this section.

So if order matters, it stands to reason that if we transform the order of a data stream, we can make it more compressible.

The simplest reordering here is to simply sort our data. For example, converting [9,2,1,3,4,8,0,6,7,5] to [0,1,2,3,4,5,6,7,8,9] makes it possible for us to delta encode it as [0,1,1,1,1,1,1,1,1,1], which has a lower entropy than the source.

Sadly though, pure sorts are one-directional. That is, after you sort the data, you can't get it back into its unsorted form without a ton of extra information to specify where it goes.

So we can't purely sort our data, but we can get close.

BWT shuffles the data stream and attempts to cluster groups of the same symbol near one another, which is what we call a *lexicographical permutation*. Or rather, with BWT you can find a permutation of the original data set that might be more compressible based on its ordering.

And here's the best part: we can encode to and decode from BWT without having to add significant additional data to our stream. Let's take a look.

How BWT Works

The "transform" part of Burrows–Wheeler transform begins by creating a table with all the shifted permutations of the input stream.

For example, we have the word BANANA, again, and write that in the first row of our table. Then, on each following line we perform a rotational shift to the right by one character of that word. That is, shift all the letters over to the right, and prepend the rightmost character at the front. We continue with this shifting, until we've touched each letter in our input string, as shown here:

BANANA

ABANA*N*

*N*ABANA

ANABA*N*

*N*ANABA

ANANA*B*

*B*ANANA

Next, the BWT algorithm sorts this table lexicographically by the bolded letters as shown in the example that follows. Feels good to have things back in order, doesn't it?

ABANA*N*

ANABA*N*

ANANA*B*

BANAN*A*

NABAN*A*

NANAB*A*

Now, we want to draw your attention to the last column of characters in the preceding example (highlighted in italics). From top to bottom, they form the string NNBAAA, which interestingly enough, is a permutation of BANANA, and has a much better clustering of letters.

And this is exactly the permutation that we're looking for. You see, by generating our rotated permutations and then lexicographically sorting them, the final column generally produces a permutation with a better symbol clustering than the original source string.

As such, NNBAAA is what BWT should return as its output.

But before you run off, there's one other piece of data we need to grab as well. Notice in the sorted table that follows, that the input string sits at index 3.

0   ABANAN

1   ANABAN

2   ANANAB

3   BANANA

4   NABANA

5   NANABA

We'll need that row index during the decode phase of the BWT transform because it will allow us to bridge from our more-compressible permutation back to the source string.

Inverse BWT

The remarkable thing about the BWT is not that it generates a more compressible output—an ordinary sort could do that—but that this particular transform is *reversible*, with minimal data overhead.

Let's illustrate this to confirm that it's true. So, we want to decode a BWT, and we're given the string NNBAAA and the row-index 3.

The first thing we need to do is regenerate the permutation table. To do this, we iterate on a combination of sorting and string appending.

We begin by writing our output string, which represents the last column, into a table.

Output string/last column
[N]
[N]
[B]
[A]
[A]
[A]

Oddly enough, if we sort this column, it is the same as the first column in our original, sorted table.[14]

Output string	Sorted
[N]	[A]
[N]	[A]
[B]	[A]
[A]	[B]
[A]	[N]
[A]	[N]

So, let's merge these two columns to get a pair of letters for each row:

[NA]

[NA]

---

14 This is not just because BANANA is an oddly shaped word. It's an observed property of BWT that we exploit, and even the BWT authors don't know why it exists.

[BA]
[AB]
[AN]
[AN]

Let's sort that:

[AB]
[AN]
[AN]
[BA]
[NA]
[NA]

Next, we prepend the original output string (NNBAAA) to it again:

[NAB]
[NAN]
[BAN]
[ABA]
[ANA]
[ANA]

Then, we sort again and continue prepending and sorting columns, until the width of the matrix equals the length of the output string.

3	4	5	6	7	8	9	10
[ABA]	[NABA]	[ABAN]	[ABAN]	[NABAN]	[ABANA]	[NABANA]	**[ABANAN]**
[ANA]	[NANA]	[ANAB]	[ANAB]	[NANAB]	[ANABA]	[NANABA]	**[ANABAN]**
[ANA]	[BANA]	[ANAN]	[ANAN]	[BANAN]	[ANANA]	[BANANA]	**[ANANAB]**
[BAN]	[ABAN]	[BANA]	[BANA]	[ABANA]	[BANAN]	[ABANAN]	**[BANANA]**
[NAB]	[ANAB]	[NABA]	[NABA]	[ANABA]	[NABAN]	[ANABAN]	**[NABANA]**
[NAN]	[ANAN]	[NANA]	[NANA]	[ANANA]	[NANAB]	[ANANAB]	**[NANABA]**

You should immediately notice two amazing properties of this final matrix:

- This final matrix is identical to the post-sorted permutation matrix that we generated in the encoder. This means that if we're given the final column of our sorted matrix, NNBAAA, we can recover the entire post-sorted matrix that was used to generate it.

- Remember that row index 3 that we output during the encoding phase? Because this matrix is identical to the post-sorted one from the encoder, we simply need to look at the row at that index the fourth row to recover our source input string BANANA.

Practical Implementations

Be warned!

Even with all this wonderfulness, sadly you can't just execute BWT on your entire 50 GB file. The way this permutation transform works, you'd have to store that same 50 GB, shifted left one symbol, for each row. That's an awful lot of extra gigabytes.

As such, BWT is what we call a block sorting transform. It breaks the file into 1 MB chunks and applies the algorithm to each of them independently. The result is an algorithm that can practically fit in the memory of most modern devices and is somewhat performant.

BWT and DNA

BWT has always been an edge-case of compression. Its initial existence showed really good results for text-based data, but it could never compete from a performance perspective with other algorithms such as GZIP. As such, BWT (or bzip2, the dominant BWT encoder) never really took the compression world by storm.

That is, until humans began sequencing deoxyribonucleic acid, or DNA.

Human DNA has a pretty simple setup with only four basic nucleotide bases, labeled A, C, G, and T. A given genome is basically a massive string containing these four symbols in various orderings. How much? Well, the human genome contains about 3.1647 *billion* DNA base pairs.

It turns out that BWT's block-sorting algorithm is an ideal transform that could be applied to DNA (*http://bit.ly/29H7CUQ*) to make it more compressible, searchable, and retrievable. (There's actually a boat-load of papers proving this.) The reduction in size and availability for fast reads are of high importance when aligning reads of new genomes against a reference.

This just goes to show how there's no single silver bullet when it comes to data compression. Each stream of information has its own variable characteristics and responds differently to different transforms and encoders. Although BWT might not have taken the web away from its cousin, GZIP, it stands alone as an important factor in the next few decades of bioinformatics.

Compressing BWT

So, it's apparent that BWT doesn't actually compress the data, it just transforms it. To practically use BWT, you need to apply another transform that is going to yield a stream with lower entropy, and then compress that.

The most common algorithm is to take the output of BWT and pass it to MTF, which is then followed by a statistical encoder. That's basically the inner workings of BZIP2 (*https://en.wikipedia.org/wiki/Bzip2*), folks.

Why not RLE?

Why use MTF instead of RLE? Remember that RLE is very sensitive to disruptions in runs. BWT doesn't produce enough contiguous long runs to ensure optimal RLE transform. MTF is more tolerant to this type of problem.

Why not LZ?

Why can't we use, say, LZ for this data? Well, let's take a look at a simple example. Remember that LZ works best when it can find duplicate symbol groupings for long chains.

TOBEORNOTTOBEORTOBEORNOT works well because TOBEORNOT is the longest duplicated symbol found. However, this doesn't work too well for runs of similar symbols.

Consider that if we ended up with "OBTTTTTTOOEER":

1. The LZ algorithm would look at the first T and encode it as a literal.

2. The second T would be encoded as a previous reference of 1, and length of one.

3. The third T will look ahead 1 and encode the TT pair as a previous ref of 2, and length of two. The result, is that our 6 "T" values would generate: Literal T,<-1,1>,<-2,2>,<-2,2> as tokens.

Later on, if we hit a stride of "T" values again, we can hope for a long stride match; but sadly, because BWT groups these symbols so far apart, the distance reference would be quite large, which will affect how we encoded that stream.

CHAPTER 9

Data Modeling

Anyone who's played the game "telephone" knows how important context is to the human brain. The words "cup" and "cop" taken by themselves are pretty likely to occur equally in most situations. However, if it's a loud party, and you hear a word that you believe is either "cup" or "cop," your brain will use the previous context to decide which one it was. For example, if your new friend said, "Wash the," the next word is most likely "cup." However, if they said, "Run from the", it might be "cop."[1]

This is the basic concept behind multicontext encoders. They take into account the last few observed symbols in order to identify the ideal number of bits for encoding the current symbol.

Perhaps a more concrete example is how symbol pairs influence the probability of subsequent letters in the English language.

For example, in "typical" English text, we expect to see the letter "h" about 5% of the time, on average. However, if the current symbol is a letter "t", there is a high probability, actually about 30%, that the next symbol will be "h", because the pair "th" is common in English. Similarly, the letter "u" has a general probability of about 2%. When a "q" is encountered, however, the probability is more than 99% that the next letter will be a "u". In this case, the current symbol "q" predicts that the next letter will be "u", and thus can use fewer bits assigned to it. This type of adjacency, based on stat-

---

1 But it is the Internet, so there could be a place where you're washing cops and running from cups... *shrug*

istical observance, has also dubbed this group of encoders "predictive", which you'll most likely see as the "proper" term in most official compression literature.[2]

This group can also be considered the "on-steroids" version of statistical compressors. They combine adaptive models (Chapter 3) and multiple symbol-to-codeword tables (Chapter 2) to produce the smallest codeword possible for the current symbol, based on previously observed symbols.

But this isn't a new concept. It turns out that it was first presented back in the 1700s[3] as one of the most powerful statistical computations to date.

The Chains of Markov

Markov chains are interesting creatures. Here's the super-confusing technical definition:

> A Markov chain (*https://en.wikipedia.org/wiki/Markov_chain*) is a discrete stochastic process in which the future depends only on the present and not on past history.

Given this definition, suppose for instance that we want to know the probability that a student will get an A in their math class in the fourth year of high school, and they have completed their third year. In general, we might expect that such a prediction will depend upon what grades they got in their first, second, and third years. However, if only the third (current) year had any bearing, and the grades in the previous two years could be ignored, this would be a Markov process.

Let's work out a more detailed example.

You've just completed the most awesome 104 days of summer vacation of all time. As a post-mortem,[4] you've decided to analyze how things went. You also decided to break down the analysis by days of the week. You found that on Mondays for the summer, there was a 50/50 split between activities, as shown here:

Day	Activity	Probability
Monday	Spelunking	50%
Monday	Bocce Ball	50%

---

2 Note that in every common piece of compression literature, these are called "Prediction" coders. We really don't like this terminology, because "predict" implies "can be wrong." Which seems to run counterintuitive to compression; if your encoding or decoding is wrong in predicting what symbol is next, you end up with a broken compression system. Instead, we prefer to refer to these algorithms as multicontext, in that they weave together multiple symbols and statistical tables/models in order to identify the least number of bits needed to encode the next symbol.

3 Decision support systems have a long history going back to Pascal (*https://en.wikipedia.org/wiki/Blaise_Pascal*).

4 Evaluation of summer vacation is a totally common thing to do for people that read books on compression.

You could describe this revelation in the following terms:

Given that today is Monday, there's a 50/50 probability that we'll either do spelunking, or bocce ball.

You find Tuesday has a more varied analysis.

Day	Activity	Probability
Tuesday	Lounging at the pool	10%
Tuesday	Sock hop[a]	20%
Tuesday	Mowing lawns	30%
Tuesday	Spelunking	40%

[a] It's a Thing (*https://en.wikipedia.org/wiki/Sock_hop*). Or rather, it used to be a Really Big Thing.

Tuesday has a similar form, in that you could say, "If today is Tuesday, Sock Hop has a 20% chance of being our activity."

Effectively, this is what we call a "second-order context." We take two pieces of data and use them to define the probability of an activity. The day of the week acts as our "first order" or "context-1" data, the activity responds as the "second order" or "context-2" data, and the result is our percentage probability.

So, let's try a third-order context:

Day	First activity	Second activity	Probability of second activity
Monday	Bocce Ball	Pedicures	5%
Monday	Bocce Ball	Smoothies	95%
Monday	Spelunking	SFHTML5 meetup	50%
Monday	Spelunking	Pizza	25%
Monday	Spelunking	Sewing class	25%

This example is a little more complex. Basically, "Given that today is Monday, AND we just did Bocce Ball, there's a 25% chance we're going to get some pizza."

Each context describes a transition between states, to some known depth.

You could visualize this as a tree (Figure 9-1), where each node is an activity, and each transition has a probability.

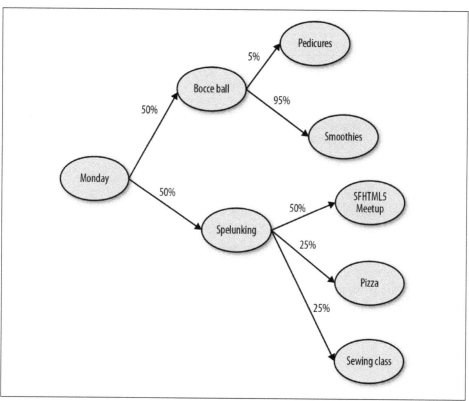

Figure 9-1. A tree diagram of how a Markov chain would work

Meet Andrey Markov

In 1913, Andrey Andreyevich Markov founded a new branch of probability theory by combining mathematics and poetry.

Delving into the text of the Alexander Pushkin (*https://en.wikipedia.org/wiki/ Alexander_Pushkin*) novel *Eugene Onegin*, Markov spent hours sifting through patterns of vowels and consonants. On January 23, 1913, he published his work, creating a statistical model detailing that, given a letter, there was a finite and reproducible probability associated with what letter would follow it.

By most accounts, Markov was a mettlesome character. He was fiercely combative with rivals, often involved in public protests and quarrels with authority, and known for spending a number of nights recovering from fisticuffs. When he published his research, he was already 50 years old and had been retired for a number of years. How fitting that the creator of one of the most powerful statistical models in history was a rebel without a cause.

Markov's concept of probabilistic event selection was massively contrary to the world of statistics at the time, which mostly involved modeling coin-flipping and dice-rolling. Markov chains help us ask questions about associated probability; for example, "If it's cloudy today, what is the probability of rain two days from now?"—a concept that in 1913 was as predictable with mathematics as it was by casting chicken bones.

Recent years have seen the construction of truly enormous Markov chains. For example, the PageRank algorithm devised by Larry Page and Sergey Brin, the founders of Google, is based on a Markov chain whose states are the pages of the World Wide Web—perhaps 40 billion of them. The transitions are links between pages. The aim of the algorithm is to calculate for each web page the probability that a reader following links at random will arrive at that page.

Amazon uses Markov chains to determine what types of recommendations to give you. For example, if other people viewed A, and then bought B, we can recommend B to you at a high percentage when you view A.

Markov chains are big in games promotion now, where a company will say, "You liked an action game before, and you've liked games about puppies, so chances are, you'll like a new action game where puppies fight alien invaders."[5]

Basically, the power of these algorithms is limitless for searching and finding, predicting weather, and matching user preference. Heck, one might even be able to predict the next military conflict (*http://bit.ly/29H7IvG*) using them!

Markov and Compression

The concept of Markov chains fits nicely into our existing models because we can view statistical encoders as single-context Markov chains. Given one table of probability for the symbols of a stream, we assign codewords accordingly.

A second-context Markov chain could be created by adding a symbol-to-codeword table for each preceding symbol, such as that illustrated in Figure 9-2. Let's see how this works.

---

5 Actually, this is the one paragraph in the book where the coauthors were not in agreement. Because, obviously, it would be cute kittens who saved the day.

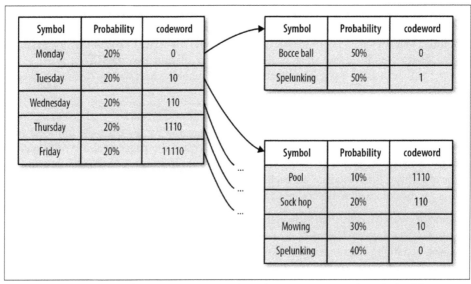

Symbol	Probability	codeword
Monday	20%	0
Tuesday	20%	10
Wednesday	20%	110
Thursday	20%	1110
Friday	20%	11110

Symbol	Probability	codeword
Bocce ball	50%	0
Spelunking	50%	1

Symbol	Probability	codeword
Pool	10%	1110
Sock hop	20%	110
Mowing	30%	10
Spelunking	40%	0

Figure 9-2. A second-order or 2-context Markov chain uses a tree of symbol tables, as could be built for our summer vacation example.

Given the graph in Figure 9-2, to encode "Monday, Spelunking; Tuesday, Pool" we'd produce 0 1 10 1110 for a total of 8 bits. In contrast, if we were to enumerate each of the 10 states, we'd end up with something along the lines of 12+ bits to encode the same data.

From a technical standpoint, creating Markov chains for compression follows many of the rules we covered in adaptive statistical encoding (see Chapter 2); that is, reading in a symbol, dynamically updating a frequency table, and so on.

Encoding

For example, let's create a Markov chain for the string "TOTOTO".

1. We begin by creating a context-1 table containing the <literal> symbol only at 100% probability.

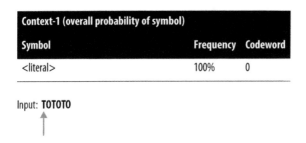

Context-1 (overall probability of symbol)		
Symbol	Frequency	Codeword
<literal>	100%	0

Input: **TOTOTO**

2. We read our first symbol, which is "T" and a new symbol.

3. We update the context-1 table to include "T" and adjust probabilities.

Context-1		
Symbol	Frequency	Codeword
T	50%	1
\<literal\>	50%	0

4. We output \<literal\> and "T".

Stream: 0 T

Input: TOTOTO

5. We read the next symbol from the stream, which is "O" and a new symbol.

6. We update context-1 to include "O" and updated probabilities.

7. We adjust the codewords to account for all symbols and satisfy the prefix property.

Context-1		
Symbol	Frequency	Codeword
T	33%	0001
0	33%	001
\<literal\>	33%	01

8. We output \<literal\> and "O".

Stream: 0 T 01 0

Input: TOTOTO

9. We read the next symbol from the stream, which is "T" and already in context-1.

10. We update context-1 to reflect the changed probabilities.

11. We swap the codewords so that the shortest one is for the symbol with the highest probability.

Context-1		
Symbol	Frequency	Codeword
T	50%	01
0	25%	001
<literal>	25%	0001

12. We output the codeword for "T" to the stream, which is 01.

   Stream: 0 T 01 0 **01**

   Input: TOT**OTO**

13. We read the next symbol from the stream, which is "O".

14. We update the context-1 probabilities and leave our codewords unchanged.

Context-1		
Symbol	Frequency	Codeword
T	40%	01
0	40%	001
<literal>	20%	0001

15. We output 001 to the stream.

   Stream: 0 T 01 0 01 **001**

16. We can now create the second link in our Markov chain by starting a second symbol-to-codeword table that represents the characters following a "T" value.

Context-2, following "T" probabilities		
Symbol	Frequency	Codeword
0	50%	0
<literal>	50%	1

Input: TOTO**TO**

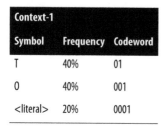

17. We read the next symbol from the stream, which is another "T".

18. We update the context-1 probabilities and leave the codewords unchanged. Context-2 for "following T" does not change.

Context-1		
Symbol	Frequency	Codeword
T	33%	01
0	33%	001
<literal>	33%	0001

19. We output 01.

   Stream: 0 T 01 0 01 001 **01**

20. We can now build a context-2 table for symbols following "O".

Context-2, following 0 probabilities		
Symbol	Frequency	Codeword
T	100%	0

   Input: TOTOT**O**

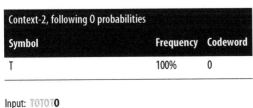

21. We read the final symbol, which is "O".

22. We can now take advantage of the context-2 table created for "following T" and output 0 as our final symbol.

   Final stream: 0 T 01 0 01 001 01 **0**

And voilá, compression!

Decoding

To prove that this is reversible and works, let's decode our stream:

1. Read 0. We know this is the literal symbol, so we build our context-1 table with it (100%).

0 T 01 0 01 001 01 0

2. Read "T". Literal. Add this to context-1 and adjust probabilities (50/50).

   Output: T

3. Read "01". According to context-1, this announces another literal.
4. Read "O". Update context-1 (33/33/33).

   Output: O

5. Read "01". According to context-1, this is "T". Update context-1 (50/25/25).

   Output: T

6. Read "001". According to context-1, this is "O". Update context-1 (40/40/20).

   Output: O

7. Build context-2 for following "T".
8. Read "01", which is "T". Update context-1 (33/33/33).

   Output: T

9. Build context-2 for following "O".
10. Read "0". Preceding context is "T", looking 0 up in context-2 "following T", we get "O".

    Output: O

And there you have it.

You can do the same thing with more symbols and longer strings, and as you can see, it gets pretty complex pretty fast.

Compression

For all that complexity, how do we win in terms of compression?

When applied to compression, Markov makes it possible for you to encode adjacent symbols with fewer bits.

Look at the two context-2 tables. They both contain 0, the shortest possible encoding. Because we are using the preceding symbol as disambiguation context, we can use the same short VLC twice, thus saving bits. Another way of saying this is that each context has its own VLC space, and thus we can use the same VLC.

After we have more symbols and longer input streams, we can build up multiple contexts. Using the English language as an example, T could be a context, with H following, and TH could be another context, with E, I, U, O, and A following.

Although U on its own has a frequency of 2.7% (*https://en.wikipedia.org/wiki/ Letter_frequency*), which would assign it a pretty long code, in the particular context of "following Q", it would get a much shorter code.

And this makes Markov chains exceptionally powerful.

Practical Implementations

It's worth pointing out that no one really uses Markov chains for compression. At least not in the way just described.

Consider a worst-case—but not implausible—scenario, in which you have an 8-context chain.

This means that for each node, you're going to end up with 256 other child nodes, 8 deep. This means that you will need 256^8 (two-hundred-fifty-six-to-the-power-of-eight!) or 16 *exabytes* of memory[6] to represent your tables. Which is crazy, even by modern computing standards.[7] As such, various derivative algorithms have been created that are just a little more practical about memory and performance than a general Markov chain. The most notable ones are *prediction by partial matching* and *Context Mixing*, which we are going to take a look at next.

Prediction by Partial Matching

A practical implementation of Markov is all about understanding memory and quickly being able to encode the most optimal chain. A memory- and computationally efficient approach to Markov chains was created by John Cleary and Ian Witten back in 1984,[8] called *prediction by partial matching* (PPM). Much like Markov chains,

---

6 Or 17,179,869,184 GB.

7 This sentence was written in 2015, when dual-core mobile devices ruled the earth like vengeful gods.

8 J. Cleary, and I. Witten, "Data Compression Using Adaptive Coding and Partial String Matching," IEEE Transactions on Communications 21:4 (1984): 390–402.

PPM uses an N-symbol context to determine the most efficient way to encode the $N + 1$th symbol.

Whereas a simple Markov implementation works in a forward manner by reading the current symbol and seeing if it's a continuation of the existing chain, PPM works in reverse. Given the current symbol in the input stream, PPM scans back N symbols and determines the probability of the current symbol from the N previous symbol context. If the current symbol has a zero probability with the N-context, PPN will try an N - 1 context. If no matches are found in any context, a fixed prediction is made.

For example:

1. Suppose that the word "HERE" has been seen several times while compressing an input stream, so context has been established.
2. Somewhere later, the encoder starts compressing "THERE" and is currently compressing the R symbol.
3. In a 3-symbol context, the previous symbols of R are "THE".
4. However, this encoder has never seen "THER", only "THE " (with a space).
5. As such, the current R has "zero probability". (That is, R hasn't been encountered before, given the previous 3–symbol context.)
6. At this point, PPM would try a 2-symbol context, attempting to match "HER" as a chain.
7. This results in a success because "HERE" has been seen many times before, which among others, created a 2-context for "HE".
8. Thus "R" has a "nonzero probability" based on the 2-context chain "HE."

Here's a more formal version:

1. The encoder reads the next symbol "S" from the input stream.
2. The encoder looks at the last N symbols read; that is, the order-N context.
3. Based on this input data that has been seen in the past, the encoder determines the probability P that "S" will appear following the particular context.
4. If the probability is zero, the encoder emits an escape token for the decoder so that the decoder can mirror the process.[9]

---

9 Yes, you're absolutely correct. This means that if a symbol has never been encountered before, PPM can emit N "escape codes" to the stream before the final literal symbol. Most of the differences between variants of this algorithm (PPMA and PPMB, PPMC, PPMP and PPMX) have to do with how they handle nuances in this escape-code process.

5. Then, the encoder repeats from step 2 with $N = N - 1$, until the probability is nonzero, or it runs out of symbols.

6. If the encoder runs out of symbol, a fixed (e.g., based on character frequency) probability is assigned.

7. The encoder then invokes a statistical encoder to encode "S" with probability P.

The Search Trie

The main problem with any practical implementation of PPM has to do with the creation of a data structure where all contexts (0 through N) of every symbol read from the input stream are stored and can be located quickly. In simplistic cases, this can be implemented with a special tree data structure called a trie,[10] for which each branch represents a context.

For example, let's build a PPM trie for the string "ABAC", with a maximum[11] allowed context of 2, as depicted in Figure 9-3.

1. Reading in the first value, "A", appends a new node [A,1] to the root of the tree. This represents that "A" has been seen 1 time so far at context 1. (Children of the root node are context 1, grandchildren are context 2, and so on).

2. Reading the second value, "B", adds two nodes to the tree.

    a. First, it adds an order-1 context node, [B,1]. This is useful in the case where "B" is the start of its own context chain.

    b. Second, it adds an order-2 context node [B,1] under the [A,1] node. This is to represent the chain "AB" that we've read through the input stream so far.

3. Reading the next "A" value has a few tricks.

    a. First, it updates the count value of the order-1 context node, (because "A" has already been encountered at that context).

    b. Next, it adds an [A,1] node as a child of each [B,1] nodes. This represents both the order 1 and order 2 contexts of "BA" and "ABA", respectively.

4. The final symbol, "C" follows a similar process, but with a small change.

    a. We add the order-1 context node [C,1].

    b. The next step would be to add 4-order [C,1] nodes to all 3-order [A,*] nodes. You can see that on the lefthand side, this is completed fine with the [B,1]-

---

10 This is the proper spelling: stick with us and find out why.

11 Limiting the number of context levels is one way of controlling complexity.

>[A,1] chain. However, on the right side, adding the new node would violate our context height restriction. So, we append nothing.

c. As a final step, we have a valid [A,1] node at order-1, and add a [C,1] node as a child there.

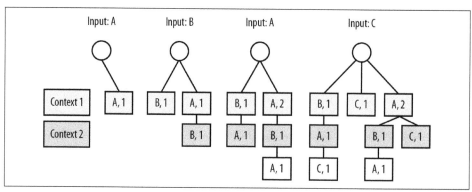

Figure 9-3. Building a PPM trie with an N-context of 2. Each level of the tree represents a context. The children of the root are the first-order context. The number next to the character denotes how many times that symbol has been encountered, at that context.

This trie is beneficial, in that we can quickly query the *N*-minus-*X* contexts, given a current state. For example, given a symbol "C", our 2-order context is "BA", our 1-order context is "A". This fits perfectly because it represents a sliding window of the previous one and two symbols from "C" in the "ABAC" string we encoded.

We can use this trie to represent all of the following substrings of the input, given a 2-context limit (Figure 9-4): B, BA, BAC, C, A, AB, AC, and ABA.

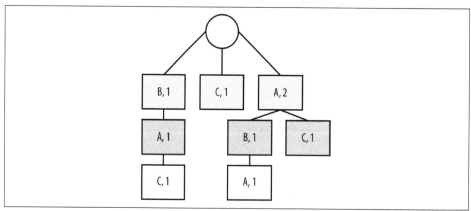

Figure 9-4. Strings represented by this trie: B, BA, BAC, C, A, AB, AC, and ABA.

Compressing a Symbol

In addition to providing efficient storage and fetching of substrings, the trie structure also contains counts per level. A statistical encoder can use these to build probability tables and assign encodings for each symbol, as shown in Figure 9-5.

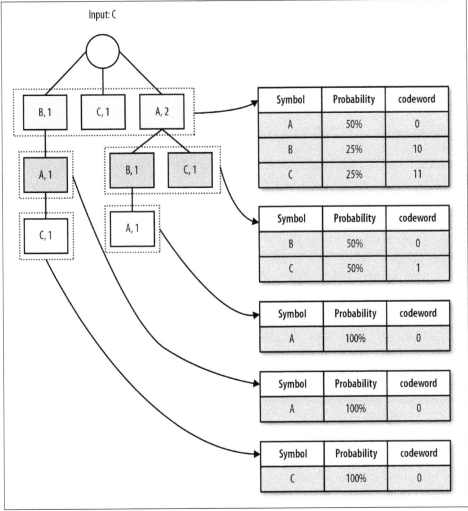

Figure 9-5. The PPM trie, and an example of the symbol-to-codeword tables you could use for encoding.

Effectively, given a level, we only need to consider the siblings at this level and normalize their values to arrive at probabilities. For example, the context-1 counts of [B, 1], [C,1], and [A,2] would represent probabilities of 25%, 25%, and 50%, respectively.

Also, note that because we can use 1-bit encodings in context-2, for every symbol encountered in context, we save 1 bit, for potentially substantial savings.

You can implement this in a straightforward fashion as a modification to the data structures we covered in Chapter 3.

Choosing a Sensible N Value

So what is the value of N supposed to be? PPM selects a value N and tries to make matches based on that context length. If no match is found, a shorter context length is chosen. As such, it seems that a long context (large value of N) would result in the best prediction. However most PPM implementations skew toward an N value of 5 or 6, trading off memory, processing speed, and compression ratio.

There are variants of PPM, such as *PPM**, which try to extend the value of N and make it exceptionally large. You can do this with a new type of trie data structure, and significantly more computational resources than PPM. This usually results in about 6% better savings than straight-up PPM.

Dealing with Unknown Symbols

Much of the work in optimizing a PPM model is handling inputs that have not already occurred in the input stream. The obvious way to handle them is to create a "never-seen" symbol which triggers the escape sequence. But what probability should be assigned to a symbol that has never been seen? This is called the *zero-frequency problem*.

One variant of PPM uses the Laplace estimator (*https://en.wikipedia.org/wiki/Laplace_operator*), which assigns the "never-seen" symbol a fixed pseudo-count of one. A variant called PPMD increments the pseudo-count of the "never-seen" symbol every time the "never-seen" symbol is used. (In other words, PPMD estimates the probability of a new symbol as the ratio of the number of unique symbols to the total number of symbols observed.)

PPMZ presents one of the more interesting variants. It starts in the same way as PPM* does, by trying to match a N-context probability for the current symbol. However, if a probability isn't found, it switches to a separate algorithm called a Local-Order-Estimator (*http://bit.ly/29H6QaF*) and uses the basic PPM model, with a completely separate predictor.

Context Mixing

Trying to improve PPM algorithms has led to the *PAQ* series of data compression algorithms—in particular, work in the PPMZ area, where multiple types of context tries are used, based on how a symbol responds to matching.

This concept evolved over time into *context missing*; that is, using two or more statistical models of the data in order to determine the optimal encoding for a given symbol. For example, using a statistical model of how often you visit "The Gym" against all your regular activities (like rescuing kittens), and another statistical model of probability of visiting "The Gym" within 12 hours of eating too much spaghetti. Given the question of "What's the probability that I will go to the gym right now?", each model will yield a different probability. Because there is a 20% chance that you go to the gym generally, and because it's been six hours since indulging in Italian cuisine, you're 50% likely to go to the gym right now. The combination of those probabilities is what context mixing is all about.

Context mixing brings two interesting questions to the table with respect to data compression:

- What types of models should you use on the data?
- How should you combine those models?

Types of Models

As we discussed earlier, adjacency is a very important topic to data compression. Algorithms such as LZ, RLE, delta, and BWT all work from the assumption that the adjacency of our data has something to do with the optimal way to encode it.

When introducing Markov, it's easy to present it in this same light. Creating an adjacency-based context is easy to do ("if A follows B", etc.). But in reality, this is just one way to create a contextual correlation between symbols. For instance, you might create a context as all values in an even index, or context might be derived from values which are clustered around a certain numerical range. Basically, adjacency and locality are the simplest forms of contextuality, but by no means are they the only ones.

With this mentality, it makes logical sense that there might be other signals in the data stream that could help us identify the right way to encode the current symbol, signals that have nothing to do with context or adjacency. Identifying and describing the relationships between symbols is what we call models. By modeling the data, we understand more about the various attributes it contains, and can we better describe the current symbol.

In reality, models can be anything and can change depending on the type of data you have.

For example, images care a lot about two-dimensional locality; that is, a pixel color generally has something to do with the adjacent colors above, below, and on each side of it, and we can take advantage of that for compression. This model doesn't work for text though. There's generally no observance that a character has any proper relation to one below or above it.[12]

In programming, after compiling your high-level instructions into bytecode, there's a completely separate model. A single byte can describe an instruction, followed by a set of variable-length bytes that describe the input to that function. Because code tends to have common patterns, you could model that if you see a "Jump to this instruction" command, there's most likely going to be a "push the variables onto the call stack" command around here somewhere, as well. So in this case, it's not important to note the adjacent bytes, but the commands themselves.

Music is a completely different beast. You could create models to represent the bass line, or guitar riffs, and take into account the lengths of courses or bridges that are involved.

The point here is that there's thousands of different ways to model your data if you just know enough about it to ask the right questions. So the problem becomes more difficult in some cases, because now, we're not talking about generic algorithms, but more asking the question, "Do you understand enough about your data to model it properly?"

One of the pioneering compressors in the context mixing space, PAQ, includes the following models:

- N-grams (*https://en.wikipedia.org/wiki/N-gram*). The context is the last *N* bytes before the predicted symbol (as in PPM).

- Whole-word *n*-grams, ignoring case and nonalphabetic characters (useful in text files).

- "Sparse" contexts. For example, the second and fourth bytes preceding the predicted symbol (useful in some binary formats).

- "Analog" contexts, consisting of the high-order bits of previous 8- or 16-bit words (useful for multimedia files).

- Two-dimensional contexts (useful for images, tables, and spreadsheets). The row length is determined by finding the stride length of repeating byte patterns.

- Specialized models that are only active when a particular file type is detected, such as x86 executables, or BMP (*http://bit.ly/29H6z7C*), TIFF (*https://en.wikipedia.org/wiki/TIFF*), or JPEG (*https://en.wikipedia.org/wiki/JPEG*) images.

And PAQ is no joke. It's constantly at the top of the Large Text Compression benchmark (*http://mattmahoney.net/dc/text.html*), and one of the newer versions, ZPAQ

---

12 ...unless you are compressing word games or some very wacky poetry.

(*http://mattmahoney.net/dc/zpaq.html*), attained second place in a contest compressing human DNA (*http://www.mattmahoney.net/dc/fastqz/*).

Types of Mixing

Just off the cuff, how would you mix two given values? Average them? Add them together? Maybe weigh them differently based upon user preference or prior input? And these questions become more complex as you start using multiple models. After you have a set of 50 inputs, how do you combine models to pick the best compression?

Thankfully, statistics have mostly solved this problem for us. There are two types of approaches to mixing the outputs from different models together.

Linear mixing is a process of using the weighted average of the predictions, where the value comes from the weight of the evidence.

In our previous example, we were trying to figure out the probability of you going to the gym given how often you go to the gym, and how often you eat pasta. Now, these two values have a different evidence weight, in that one might be proving a more reliable value due to more tests/samples taken. For example, if you're considering how pasta influences your gym attendance at a lifetime level, it would have more sample data and thus be a more reliable form of predictor than, say, your frequency of going to the gym in the last week.[13] As such, we give one more weight in the mixed model due to it having more evidence.

Logistic mixing, on the other hand, is crazy.

You see, with linear mixing, there's really no feedback loop to indicate to you whether the weight you assigned to a model was correct toward predicting how to compress this data. So, if your input stream changes, and the weighting of your models stays the same, you can end up bloating your output stream.

To address this, logistic mixing uses a neural network (artificial intelligence!) to update weights and reassign them based upon what models have given the most accurate predictions in the past. The trick here is with correcting the current weightings. Suppose that the current weight selects model A to encode this symbol in 12 bits. But model B would have been the correct choice, with an 8-bit encoding. The encoder outputs the 12 bits and then updates its weights so that when all of these models produce these same values next time, model B has a higher chance of being chosen.

The only downside to this is the massive amount of memory and running time it takes to compress the data. If you look at ZPAQ on the LTCB (*http://mattmaho*

---

13 We are totally going to the gym next week. We hear there's a new spin class we should check out.

ney.net/dc/text.html), it took 14 GB of memory to compress a 1 GB file. All that modeling data has to go somewhere, right?

The Next Big Thing?

Context mixing shines a light on the future of data compression. Basically, with unlimited memory and running time, combined with enough modeling knowledge of the data, optimal compression is a solved problem. This might be the next big solution to data compression at a cloud-computing level. Companies that have tons of compute resources and time to spend on them, could be able to aggressively compress data, *given that their data-science team has properly identified all the models for it.*

But this hasn't yet made its way to the consumer market. The high overhead of memory and runtime make context mixing improbable for mobile devices (at the time of writing this book). But the reality is that it's a completely different data target. If you're only dealing with 1 MB to 50 MB of data, the results of compressing using context modeling are pretty similar to a lot of other algorithms out there. It's when your data is large, complex, and ever-changing that context mixing begins to shine.

So, this goes back to the same thing again: there's no silver bullet when it comes to compression. Each data set needs a unique thought process and analysis on how to define and approach the information. Even context modeling, which is built to adapt to the data, still relies on humans creating models for the information.

Which means there's one thing for certain: data compression is far from a solved problem, and there is so much more awesomeness left to discover there.

CHAPTER 10

Switching Gears

Until now, this book has focused mainly on specific data compression algorithms and how they generally work. Even though it's all highly informative, unless you're trying to write your own breakthrough data compressor, it's primarily useful as a foundation for understanding and compressing your data. So, we'd like to switch gears and talk about the pragmatic points of data compression, and how they relate to you, the projects you develop, and the world at hand.

There are two types of compression out there right now: *media-specific* and *general-purpose*. Let's look at each of them.

Media-Specific Compression

Media specific compressors are designed specifically for media data such as images, audio, video, and the like. Most likely, these types of files and compressors make up the majority of content your applications send, receive, manipulate, store, and display to users. The old saying, "A picture is worth a thousand words," is quite literally true when it comes to data compression: a 1024 x 1024 RGB image is 3 MB of data. If you assume ASCII-encoded letters, you could display 3,145,728 letters for that same size. To put that into context, the famous book *The Hobbit* is made up of 95,022 words. If you assume an average word size of 5 letters, that's roughly 475,110 characters. You could fit that book about 6 times into a single 1024 × 1024 image.

This is why most media compressors employ *lossy* compression algorithms. Lossy compression algorithms are types of data transforms that reduce the quality of the media in an attempt to make the content more compressible. For example, a 1024 × 1024 image, using 8 bits each for the red, green, and blue channels, comes to 24 bits per pixel, and hence 3 MB. However, if you used only 4 bits per channel, you'd end up with 12 bits per pixel, bringing the total footprint to 1.5 MB, while also reducing the color-quality of the image.[1]

There is an unending horde of lossy data-transforms out there, each one specialized for a specific media type (what works on images won't work nearly as well on audio) and content type (grayscale images can use a different compressor than full-color images). Ignoring that the transforms are lossy, media-specific compressors pretty much follow what we have discussed so far. After the content is transformed into a more compressible state, you can apply all the standard transforms, such as LZ, BWT, RLE, Delta compression, and even Huffman/arithmetic/ANS. The trick is (again) finding the right transforms for the right type of data to produce the best results.

We haven't spent much time talking about lossy transforms in this book. That's intentional. There are so many of these transforms, and each one is so content-specific, that you'd really need a book per mediatype.[2] But don't worry, Chapter 12 covers some important details of how you can optimize your image compression, without having to go too deep into the details.

General-Purpose Compression

General-purpose compressors, on the other hand, are built for everything else. These are algorithms like DEFLATE (*https://en.wikipedia.org/wiki/DEFLATE*), GZIP (*https://en.wikipedia.org/wiki/Gzip*), BZIP2 (*https://en.wikipedia.org/wiki/Bzip2*), LZMA (*http://bit.ly/28KCeka*), and PAQ (*https://en.wikipedia.org/wiki/PAQ*), which combine various lossless transforms to produce savings for nonmedia files like text, source code, serialized data, and other binary content that won't tolerate lossy data compression. There's a healthy amount of research in this area. Stopping by the Large Text Compression Benchmark (*http://mattmahoney.net/dc/text.html*) shows a gaggle of general-purpose compressors that have all been tasked with compressing huge text files, to measure how they stack up against each other. And new algorithms continue to be developed. Google's stabs at improving the GZIP algorithm produced a family of compressors called Snappy (*https://en.wikipedia.org/wiki/Snappy_(software)*), Zopfli (*https://en.wikipedia.org/wiki/Zopfli*), Gipfeli (*https://github.com/google/gipfeli*), and Brotli (*https://en.wikipedia.org/wiki/Brotli*),[3] with each one focusing on either better compression, lower memory requirements, or faster decompression.

---

1 We are basically reducing the number of possible colors from about 16 million to 4,096. The human eye can distinguish more than a million colors. For more on this, see the Wikipedia entry "Trichromacy" (*https://en.wikipedia.org/wiki/Trichromacy*).

2 Not convinced? Go read up on how the JPG format (*https://en.wikipedia.org/wiki/JPEG*) works, or brush up on the new WebM format (*https://www.youtube.com/watch?v=K6JshvblIcM*).

3 Basically, a Swiss bakery shop of algorithms.

Most of the Internet content you download each day has been compressed with one of these algorithms. The standard HTTP stack allows for data packets to be encoded with GZIP, BZIP, and now, Brotli compressors (as long as the server and client support it), which means webpages, JavaScript files, tweets, and store listings are most likely showing up on your device after being decompressed.

It's worth pointing out that many in the compression community, including the authors of this book, believe that these algorithms are caught in a race to a point of diminishing returns. Looking at the most recent, successful encoders (Brotli, LZHAM (*https://github.com/richgel999/lzham_codec*), LZFSE (*http://apple.co/28MjogJ*), ZSTD (*http://bit.ly/28KBN9C*)), they all show a similar trend: minor variations on a theme. New tricks and modifications to existing transforms are applied to existing algorithm types in order to get small savings in compression. And they require more resources to begin producing marginal savings. Looking at various benchmarks (*https://quixdb.github.io/squash-benchmark/*), we're not seeing breakthroughs in 30%–50% savings; rather, lots of sweat and effort is being expended to get 2%–10% improvement over existing algorithms.

Compression in Practice

We hope that with all the awesome knowledge in this book, applying all of this to the development of your applications will be pretty straightforward. But there are a few things we specifically want to cover, which can help you understand more about addressing the lowest-hanging fruit in your application development. The next few chapters will focus on understanding how to evaluate various types of data compression options, and then give you some tips on images and serialized data, followed by some bigger-picture thinking about the importance of data compression over the next decade.

Fun stuff!

CHAPTER 11

Evaluating Compression

Before bounding off into the weeds and jamming compression into every part of your fancy application, it's important to note all of the trade-offs and use cases involved. Not every algorithm is suited for every use case, and in some instances, a different implementation of the same compression format might better match your need.

So, when it comes to data compression, what matters?

Compression Usage Scenarios

Let's begin this discussion by setting the stage on where data is compressed, stored, and decompressed. This is critical for understanding where the data is coming from and where it's going, because of the important interplay between encoder and decoder, which we'll talk about more in a bit. First, let's look at four common scenarios.

Compressed Offline, Decompressed On-Client

In this first scenario, the data is compressed somewhere unrelated to the client, and then distributed to the client, where it's decompressed for use.

This scenario is most common for things like packaged applications or video games, and the resources often include copious amounts of images, videos, and music. Another use case is artists creating and sharing their work. In both cases, the original art is created by using high-resolution, high-fidelity tools, and then exported and compressed for distribution.

Compression aims to optimize for the smallest possible media files.

The trade-off is one of quality.

Compressed On-Client, Decompressed In-Cloud

Most modern social media applications generate a lot of content on the client and then push it up to the cloud for processing and distribution to other fellow social users. In these situations, some mild compression is usually done on the client, in order to reduce the amount of overhead in the outbound communication. For example, taking a packet of social data, and serializing it with a binary serialization format, and then gzip compressing it before sending it up to the server.

The primary goal here is to reduce cost for the user. Although many in North America (still) have the benefit of being on an unlimited data plan,[1] much of the rest of the world doesn't enjoy this luxury, so most clients are on pay-for-transfer plans. This means that every bit they transfer to the server is paid for by them.

The trade-off is that on mobile, you spend battery resources compressing this data.

Compressed In-Cloud, Decompressed On-Client

Data that is compressed in the cloud falls into two primary buckets, which have entirely different characteristics.

Dynamic data that is generated by the cloud resource

On the flip-side of users sending data to the cloud is data that originates in the cloud that the user downloads.

For example, when a client requests the results of some database operation, or the server sends dynamic layout data, the client is waiting for content to be generated. The time it takes for the server to generate and compress that data is critically important; otherwise, the client will experience network latency.

What's essential here is balancing size and compression time. It is worth pointing out that in some high-latency environments, users might be willing to wait the extra time in return for a smaller payload.

Compression aims to minimize what's being sent over the network.

The trade-off is one of time.

Large data that's passed off to the cloud for efficient computing

The importance in this scenario is often pushed toward ensuring minimization of bits for the medium at hand. For example, imagine having two gigabytes of PNG files that

---

1 This is changing while we are writing this book.

need to be converted to WebP images at 10 different resolutions, or 1,200 hours of video that must be converted to H.264 before being displayed.

Remember every bit sent from the cloud must be paid for by the cloud owner, and in effect, each bit that the client has to consume from the cloud also has to be paid for by the client. Using cloud-compute resources is ideal in situations for which you want to minimize those bits in the most compute-effective way possible.

The goal is to efficiently compress large amounts of data into the fewest possible bits.

The trade-off is one of cost versus efficiency (that is, the price of compute resources.)

Compressed On-Client, Decompressed On-Client

Finally, there are many client applications that need to communicate with one another. They might send peer-to-peer network packets, or photos, or GPS information.

In these cases, the client generates the data, compresses it, and then sends it to the other client to decompress.

What's difficult about these situations is that the client machine, often a mobile device, typically doesn't have the massive amount of resources required to optimally transform and compress data. However, these devices usually have specialized graphics hardware, which can be used to compress things like JPG and H.264 (*https:// en.wikipedia.org/wiki/H.264/MPEG-4_AVC*), and you end up with a win for images and video. For other types of data, this means that the quality of the data compression will be lower (due to less time available to optimize), and that the decompression time can be slower as well (due to less power on client devices).

As such, algorithms that communicate client-to-client often settle on fixed-bit compression, such as manually packing serialized structures rather than compressing them.

There isn't a trade-off as such; instead, there's a balancing act between the capabilities of the device, the time it takes to compress and decompress, and the immediacy of the need for the data.

Compression Need

As we've already hinted while exploring the different algorithms, it's exceptionally important to understand that not all compression algorithms and formats apply to all data types. For example, applying Huffman to image data won't produce the level of savings that applying a lossy image[2] compression algorithm will.

As a developer, matching the right algorithm to the right data type is critical for maximizing the compression results you want, with the trade-offs you'll need to make. And there is no silver bullet. It comes down to this:

- Know your data—not just what type of data, but also its internal structure, and in particular, how it's used.

- Know your algorithm options so that you can chose from the right family of compressors.[3]

- Most important, know what you need for the given circumstance, because you might find surprising savings there.

What does this mean in practice?

For instance, thumbnail images may be able to tolerate a lower quality level than, say, full-screen versions. As such, they could be compressed with a lossy JPEG encoder, whereas the higher-quality version should be encoded by using a lossless WebP codec.

Compression Ratio

Compression ratio, that is, the amount by which the content is compressed, is often the most important factor when evaluating compression options. Because the primary goal of compression is to produce the most compact form of the data, because the smallest number of bits on the wire will always win.

Except...there are always exceptions. You might be willing to to settle for less compression savings when performance or memory take priority. Here is a perfect example: ZPAQ (*https://en.wikipedia.org/wiki/ZPAQ*) will generally produce the smallest compressed files for 1 GB text files. But it also generally requires around 2 GB of memory and 3 hours to compress this on a desktop machine, and similarly for decompression. So yes, ZPAQ is a great when it comes to file size, but it's not very applicable to compressing data on a mobile device.

Now, for services that can do compression offline, or in the cloud, compression ratio is one of the most important considerations. You do have the extra resources and

---

2 Algorithms that lose information during the compression process. See Chapter 14 for some words on lossy compression.

3 More specifically, algorithms that work for blocks of text might not compress numerical data well, and vice versa.

time for compressing your data to its smallest form, and there is cold, hard cash involved in sending around the bits.

Users Get the Short End

It's worth pointing out that users always get the short end of the stick in this equation. Most of the world isn't on "unlimited data" plans, and the cost for the users to bring down 1 GB of data, compared to the cost for someone to serve 1 GB of data, are monumentally different.

If you want to build an app that keeps users happy, try to shoulder the cost of transfer on behalf of your users.

Compression Performance

Compression performance is all about how long it takes to get data into a compressed form. Compression performance is critically important in any latency-sensitive environments, whether the client is responsible for compression, or the server is compressing data for which the client is waiting.

There are generally two evaluation metrics to care about in this regard: CPU speed and memory. The CPU speed of the encoding system is important because this determines how fast the data can be compressed. And the amount of available memory matters as soon as it's very limited, as happens to be the case on mobile devices.

For example, the LZMA algorithm achieves really impressive compression results, but at the cost of large memory footprints. This makes the algorithm less than attractive to use on mobile devices, on which there might be only 256 MB of RAM available.

Most client technologies (mobile devices anyway) have built-in support for hardware compressor codecs (coder-decoder technology), at least for some lossy data types. Things like JPG and H.264 are easily transferred to hardware, and as such, client-side compression here is easier than on servers, which typically don't have that specialized hardware.

On the lossless side, we've even seen a few GZIP chips out there, too. Because these are dedicated hardware components, they tend to be lightning fast compared to their software implementation counterparts, and you should take advantage of them any chance you get. Remember that client-side compression has much more limited resources, and if you can shift around your strategy to optimize for this performance, it usually results in a net win. Especially in places where serialized data that has to be sent around for peer-to-peer (P2P) networking, updating packet and position data every frame results in a load of data, and utilizing GZIP hardware can result in large wins.

Decompression Performance

For any performance-sensitive environments, decompression speed is the metric that rules all things. In modern application development, decompression is usually done on a client device that is quite underpowered compared to its server-side counterparts. Compression algorithms that can produce the smallest size can also come with the penalty of taking the longest time to decompress, and that makes them unusable if the data is sent to mobile devices.

The trade-off then, is that sometimes you must choose a compression algorithm based upon its decompression performance rather than just its compressed size. For example, ZPAQ, a very efficient compressor, uses a neural net as its codec and thus requires an enormous amount of runtime resources to decompress. Such requirements make it off-limits for mobile devices with smaller CPUs and battery constraints.

The WebP image format (*https://developers.google.com/speed/webp/?hl=en*) is another perfect example of this. The first few versions of WebP boasted better-quality images at smaller data sizes than JPG, but the decoding speed was almost doubled. Because of this, many companies hesitated to adopt the format. Performance improved in later versions, and mass adoption eventually happened.

Hardware decoders, which are common in laptops and mobile devices, are picking up some of the slack. Hardware JPG, OGG (*https://en.wikipedia.org/wiki/Ogg*), and H. 264 chips are boosting decode performance for their specific algorithms, making them a preferred choice under some circumstances.

Decode performance is actually one of the dominant reasons why GZIP is one of the most common archival compression algorithms on the planet right now. GZIP produces good general compression sizes at really fast decompression speeds, making it applicable for all sorts of embedded and nonembedded devices. Over the past 20+ years since its creation, the GZIP algorithm has constantly been improved to take decompression performance to new levels.

Ability to Decode-Stream

Data streaming is often an overlooked aspect of decompression. We generally think of compression algorithms as working with a "whole package," meaning that all the data needs to be in memory before any decoding can occur.

But that's actually far from the truth. Think of listening to an entire opera or watching Kenneth Branagh's *Hamlet* in one session: taking in all of it at once can be too much —better to process parts of it at a time.

Luckily, some general compression algorithms, such as GZIP, BZIP2, alongside most media compressors, like H.264, also work in a streaming mode. Data can be sent to the client in chunks that are decoded as they arrive (i.e., block encoding). For many client-side applications, this ability is highly sought after. Imagine a user scrolling through the beginning of a social media stream, and having to download the last 10 years of "what I ate for breakfast today" posts before being able to decode the "I finally planked (*https://en.wikipedia.org/wiki/Planking_(fad)*) Stonehenge" announcement.

Comparing Compressors

There are so many compression formats and algorithms out there, it's sometimes good to get them in a head-to-head battle to see which ones win on a given type of data.

Fortunately, you don't have to do this yourself. For example, the Large Text Compression Benchmark (*http://mattmahoney.net/dc/text.html*) regularly pits algorithms head-to-head for 1 GB files of text data. The Squash Compression Benchmark (*https://quixdb.github.io/squash-benchmark/*) tests various types of XML, text, images, and other data formats. And Squeeze Chart (*http://squeezechart.com/index.html*) compares all sorts of text, audio, and bitmap content.

The main point of all this is that various compressors with various settings will influence the amount of compression quality your app can take advantage of. So, in all cases, try to test a handful of options based upon your restrictions and goals, and pick the right one for you.

The "Weissman Score"

I gotta hand it to Mike Judge (*https://en.wikipedia.org/wiki/Mike_Judge*), who really helped out the compression industry. Since the 1980s, attention and gains in compression have been relatively small and slow. Sure, we had BWT in the '90s, and LZMA in the '00s, and ZPAQ in the '10s, but other than that, it's been pretty quiet. However, in a single burst of laughter, suddenly the nerd world is interested in compression again. What happened?

In 2014, the TV show *Silicon Valley* (*https://en.wikipedia.org/wiki/Silicon_Valley_(TV_series)*) burst onto the scene with much hilarity. The show follows a programmer's journey into the startup world as he tries to build a company around a revolutionary new compression algorithm. While satire, at its core, the impact on the compression community has been pretty amazing. Suddenly, it's cool to care about compression again. The media has been eating it up, and any story of a company (*http://bit.ly/28KJmwJ*) doing something interesting (*http://bit.ly/28KJlsA*) with compression (*http://bit.ly/28KJpIV*) immediately gets compared to the TV show. So when

Google released a new algorithm (*http://bit.ly/28KJpZs*), the media took the opportunity to discuss art, imitating life, imitating art, and all that jazz.

Although the compression algorithm presented in the show is all fiction, the producers wanted to have a hint of truth in things, so they contacted professor Tsachy Weissman at the University of Stanford to help them walk that line. Now, Prof. Weissman created a method for measuring the performance of data compression, which takes the compression ratio of the data set and divides it by the encoding speed of the data set. The intention is to test out the performance of new compression algorithms by normalizing their ratio/encode speed by known existing encoders (like GZIP). This normalization provides some ability to compare algorithms against universal standard compressors, which can be helpful in the evaluation of the right system for the right data type.

This new metric was named in his honor (*http://bit.ly/28KJpsz*) by the show creators as the Weissman Score (*http://bit.ly/28KJsV4*), and since has become the stuff of legend on the Internet, although it's not clear whether the score has found roots in practical use in the compression world. (Or, at least no one on encode.ru seems to be using it yet...)

The takeaway here is that with a great new attention in the data compression space, we're hopeful to see a new generation of algorithms and research focused on this area to help move compression into a new generation of breakthroughs.

CHAPTER 12

Compressing Image Data Types

If you're an application developer, chances are that the bulk of your app content is actually image data. Social media streams, shopping pages, even mapping information are all image content that must be sent down to your users, *constantly*.

Image compression is a really tricky subject. The individual lossy algorithms inside the compressors are gnarly (at best) and really should not be touched. But don't lose hope. Although these compressors are mostly treated as black-box systems, there's still a lot that your development team can do to influence the size of image content, and make it smaller.

Understanding Quality Versus File Size

Typically, image compressors provide an integer parameter that lets you define a quality metric for the image.[1]

As this value gets lower, so does the file size—and the image quality.

You see, this value mostly controls how aggressive the lossy algorithms are in transforming the data for better compression. So, lower quality means that more colors are discarded or more edge information is ignored, all to generate more duplicate symbols for subsequent statistical encoding stages.

Choosing the value for this quality metric should be a huge, important, time-consuming decision. Picking a value that is too low results in bad image artifacts, and users might complain about a lack of quality. Picking a value that is too high means

---

1 You might recognize this concept: when you save a JPG file out of Photoshop, it usually asks you what "quality level" you want.

you're sending around larger files than you need to, and paying the cost for that as well. Figure 12-1 illustrates this progression.

Figure 12-1. A set of images with different quality compression ratios—high, medium, and low; as the image size becomes smaller, the image quality degrades as well.

For small numbers of images, an artist or designer can pick the value of the quality metric manually. When they export the images from their tools, they can typically slide around the quality metric and find the right balance between image quality and final file size.

But this absolutely does not scale. If you have got 15 million users who upload pictures of their food creations to your backend, you can't employ an army of artists to find that sweet spot. What's worse: that sweet spot changes for each image. A really smooth icon or picture of a sunset will need a different quality value than a picture of a forest or someone's face. The human brain is really tricky like that, and notices image quality errors differently in different types of situations.

So, the million-dollar question is: how do you find the right value, per image, at scale?

Sadly, most developers today don't attempt to approach that problem and end up choosing one quality setting that they apply to all images in their service.

As the imgmin project (*https://github.com/rflynn/imgmin*) points out, there's generally only a small change in user-perceived quality for JPG compression between levels 75 and 100:

> For an average JPEG, there is a very minor, mostly insignificant change in "apparent" quality from 100–75, but a significant file size difference for each step down. This means that many images look good to the casual viewer at quality 75, but are half as

large than they would be at quality 95. As quality drops below 75, there are larger apparent visual changes and reduced savings in file size.

And imgmin further goes to show that most large websites tend to oscillate their images around this quality of 75 mark for almost all of their JPG images:

Company image	JPG quality
Google Images thumbnails	74–76
Facebook full-size images	85
Yahoo frontpage JPGs	69–91
YouTube frontpage JPGs	70-82
Wikipedia images	80
Windows Live backgrounds	82
Twitter user JPG images	30–100

The issue here is that the values chosen aren't ideal. They are usually the result of a single quality value chosen in a vacuum and then applied to all images coming through the system. In reality, some images could be compressed further with negligent quality loss, whereas other images will be compressed too much and not look good.

What Reduces Image Quality?

The human eye is pretty sensitive to a number of things when viewing images, including edges and gradients.[2]

Any time there's an error with an edge between two known values, or a mismatch in what the brain thinks a smooth color should look like, it's pretty noticeable (see Figure 12-2).

---

2 When we look at a picture, we intuitively know whether it's good quality (*https://en.wikipedia.org/wiki/Image_quality*). So, while "quality" is kinda fuzzy, it includes stuff such as color accuracy, sharpness, contrast, and distortion. But what we really want is to be able to measure that quality, and we'll get to that in just a minute.

Figure 12-2. A gradient image at full smoothness (left) and compressed (right). The source image has almost 128 unique colors, whereas the compressed version has only 32. This lack of unique colors creates what is called "banding," and it reduces the smooth quality of gradient images.

Quantization and *blocking* are some of the most common forms of image compression that result in visual issues. Most image compression algorithms break the data into blocks of pixels, quantized to reduce the number of unique colors involved in an image, and then make modifications based on locality of the image.

For example, JPG will group pixels into 8 x 8 blocks and attempt to find similar colors for that region. This works, because image data tends to have local regions of interest. That is, in a truly random image, there would be no correlation between two adjacent pixels; however, in a photograph, there tend to be gradients and similar colors. The result of this blocking process is that adjacent blocks might not share the same colors, and edges will be visible between the blocks, as demonstrated in Figure 12-3.

Figure 12-3. A close up of the Lena image that demonstrates the effect of blocking arti-facts.

In fact, there's an entire subset of research in understanding the types of visual arti-facts that can result from compression (*https://en.wikipedia.org/wiki/Compres sion_artifact*).

Measuring Image Quality

Although the human brain can instinctively notice and define bad image quality, it doesn't help when you're trying to automate the process of determining whether a compressor is "good." As such, it's important to have a mathematical, measurable, and thus programmable concept of "image quality."

Today, there are two competing ratios that tend to be used for evaluating image data: *peak signal-to-noise ratio* and *structural similarity*.

Peak signal-to-noise ratio (*https://en.wikipedia.org/wiki/Peak_signal-to-noise_ratio*) (PSNR), in general terms, expresses the relationship between the maximum possible power of a signal and the power of corrupting noise that affects the fidelity of its rep-resentation (in logarithmic decibel scale). This measurement is built on the *mean-square error* (MSE) of the compressed image. Or rather, how much the values of the original image differ from the compressed image.

PSNR and the MSE term work in inverse relationship. When the amount of error is low, quality (and thus PSNR) will be high, and vice versa. The only catch here is that if you try to compute the MSE between two identical images, the value will be zero and hence the PSNR will be undefined (division by zero).

But there are a few problems with the PSNR measurement. Because it computes the mean-squared reconstruction error after denoising it, it is slightly biased toward over-smoothed (that is, blurry) results. In plain English, this means that if part of the texture is also removed, scores can be high (ignoring that part of the image is missing). So, PSNR is not always consistent with respect to the source image or the types of effects applied to it. In addition, the PSNR metric relies strictly on numeric comparison and does not take into account any of the biological factors of the human vision system. So what looks good from a numbers perspective might exhibit substantial quality issues when viewed by a human eye.

The structural similarity (SSIM) index (*https://en.wikipedia.org/wiki/Structural_simi larity*) was developed to address the PSNR issues and take human perception into account when comparing the compression quality of images. This is done by looking at the similarity of the edges between the source and the compressed image. SSIM might look like a better quality measurement, but it is more complicated to compute.

The value of SSIM ranges from [0,1], where 1 represents that the compressed image is identical to the source image, and 0 means that there is no viable similarity between the compressed image and the source image.

The images in Figure 12-4 show the calculated MSE (PSNR) and SSIM side by side for a series of pictures.

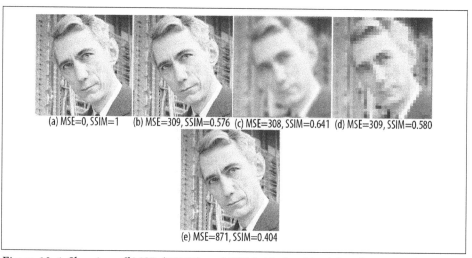

Figure 12-4. Showing off MSE (PSNR) and SSIM side by side: (a) is the original image; (b) adds white-noise to it; (c) is a blur effect; (d) is a result of low-quality JPG compression; and (e) is high-quality JPG compression. Notice how b, c, and d all have very similar MSE, despite the images being completely different from a visual perspective.

The idea here is that both PSNR and SSIM are numerical metrics that you can use to evaluate how good your image looks, post compression. This is much different than what most developers are doing, which is having an artist/designer hand-check the quality of a few samples and then choose a compression level for all of the rest of the images based on that.

Making This Work

It's apparent, then, that different types of images will require different export settings to achieve the same level of visual quality perceived by the end user. A picture of a forest will have lots of edges and unique colors, and thus will need more bits to be able to represent it adequately, whereas a hand-drawn cartoon has lots of simple colors, and thus won't create so many gradient problems. So, each image type should use a different set of export metrics. How you achieve this in your development environment is left to you, however.

Obviously, creating a cloud-compute resource to iteratively find the ideal quality is a straightforward path, but not all developers have access to the time and financial resources to achieve that.

Image Dimensions Are Important

In today's mobile world, there's a plethora of devices with many different screen sizes and varying processing power. This represents a huge problem for modern developers: What resolution should I use for my images?

Consider this: a user uploads an eight-megapixel photo from their phone.[3]

It makes sense that another user with the same screen resolution would want to see the image in the same size. But what about a user whose screen is only half or a quarter that size? This would be similar to the difference between viewing the image on a laptop monitor and a phone. Obviously, the smaller screen will display the image using fewer physical pixels because it has fewer of them to use, after all, but where should the resizing occur?

Sending the full-resolution image to the device and resizing it before rendering is certainly the easiest in terms of developer workload, but you are sending a lot of extra bits to a user who will never use them (or see them!). That's basically money thrown down the drain.

A better solution is to resize the image in your cloud, or cache a resized image somewhere so that you can send a smaller image to a smaller screen. This isn't too far-fetched a notion. Chances are, you already have the same image in multiple resolutions (Figure 12-5): a low-resolution thumbnail, a super-high one for full-

---

3 They took a picture of some Klingon blood pudding that they had for lunch.

screen, and perhaps some in between for previews. You can use automation tools, locally or in the cloud, to generate all the resolutions you need with a single invocation rather than having your artists generate them by hand in an image editor.

Figure 12-5. Image dimensions also open the door to being craftier with image quality. Fullscreen images have more visual real estate where users can identify quality problems. In smaller images, like thumbnails, you can accept a lot more quality format problems, because users might not notice or complain.

Sending appropriately sized images has multiple benefits:

- You are sending less data to your users, which is faster and respects their data plans.
- Your data takes up less space on the device, which is polite.
- No image resizing is required. (Yes, yes, we know that the GPU could do that for you, but then you're dealing with hacking a 4 MB image in GPU space, when it's only being rendered as a thumbnail.)
- Decoding is faster, loading is faster, displaying...well, you get the idea.

Choosing the Correct Image Format

As mentioned earlier, there's an entire set of different kinds of image algorithms and formats out there today. Each one has unique trade-offs and use cases that you should be aware of when developing your image compression pipeline. Let's talk about the big image formats that are used for mobile app and web development today: PNG, JPG, GIF, and WebP.

PNG

Portable Network Graphics (PNG) format (*http://bit.ly/29H5JYv*) is a lossless image format that uses a GZIP-style compressor to make its data smaller. Because the image format is lossless, the compressed image quality will be identical to your source image. This is great because you can maintain high quality while still achieving some compression, but not nearly as much compression as with lossy formats.

One of the biggest attractions of PNG is that it supports transparency. In addition to the red, green, and blue channels, it supports an alpha channel that defines which pixels to alpha-blend during rendering. This transparency support makes PNG quite attractive to the Web, and to applications where you might want an image on screen that isn't exactly rectangular. However, you are paying to have a fourth color channel, as it increases the size of your uncompressed file.

The PNG format also allows for chunks of metadata in a file. This makes it possible for image editors (and client-side devices that create images) to attach extra data to the file. Although helpful as a format, this is a common source of bloat, and most of the time, including a data chunk that describes what program exported the image, is just irrelevant junk to a user. As such, it's critically important that before sending these images around, you strip out this unneeded data.[4]

In truth, the lossless nature of the PNG file format can be a blessing and a curse. From a quality perspective, you achieve pixel-perfect results compared to your source image, but from a file-size perspective, complex images that don't contain a lot of like-colored pixels will not compress very well. If you are required to use PNG files, for example, for Android asset bundles, or a transparent image for a web page, you can improve your image compression by applying a lossy preprocess to the image file *before* you save it in the PNG format.

Thankfully for you, you won't need to write that crazy lossy preprocessing code on your own. There's a plethora of applications that will do it on your behalf. A web search for "Lossy PNG compressor" will yield more results than you'll know what to

---

4 Most photo-editing programs that export to PNG can strip out this information. There's also a plethora of PNG-specific compressors that can do that for you.

do with. Which preprocessor you choose depends heavily on your needs and the properties of your data set.

JPG

If you have no explicit need for transparency, the Joint Photographic Experts Group (JPEG or JPG for short) format (*https://en.wikipedia.org/wiki/JPEG*) will be a much better option. JPG is a format built for photographic images; it does not support alpha transparency. It contains a powerful lossy compressor that's controlled by a quality metric which lets you trade off between file size and image quality.

The compression format behind JPG is built on block encoding. As illustrated in Figure 12-6, an image is broken into small 8 × 8 blocks, and various transforms are applied to each block. The transformed blocks are then combined and thrown at a statistical encoder.

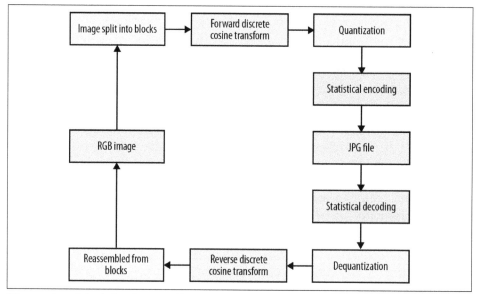

Figure 12-6. A high-level view of how the JPG algorithm works.

Blocking Is for Photos

Note that this blocking process is geared toward photographic images. If you were to compress an image with a much flatter color palette, such as a hand-drawn cartoon, the lossless compressor in PNG would perform better because it can collapse runs of similar colors into single compressed tokens.

Much like PNG, JPG files can also include metadata blocks, which means sneaky image editors or cameras can insert unneeded data into the files.[5]

JPG also brings the benefit that most mobile devices now come with hardware JPG encoders and decoders that the platforms take advantage of. This means that decode times for a JPG file can be significantly faster than for an equivalent PNG image.

GIF

GIF (*http://en.wikipedia.org/wiki/Graphics_Interchange_Format*) is another format that supports transparency, alongside with animation (which is the direct reason for the whole cats on the Internet thing (*http://bit.ly/28KNL2Q*)...). The GIF format contains two stages of compression, a lossy palletization (*http://en.wikipedia.org/wiki/Palette_(computing)*)) step that reduces the color pallette for the entire image to only 256 colors, followed by a lossless LZW (*http://en.wikipedia.org/wiki/Lempel%E2%80%93Ziv%E2%80%93Welch*) compressor. Quantizing the colors of the image down to only 256 results in an aggressive quality reduction at the benefit of better compression sizes, which tends to produce better compression from the LZW end of things. GIF tends to be pretty well supported on the Web; however, native platforms don't have uniform support for it.

WebP

The WebP format offers a middle ground between PNG and JPG. WebP supports a lossless mode and transparency as well as a lossy mode. Basically, you can choose between the best parts of JPG and PNG. Although that sounds like the Holy Grail of image formats, there are a few caveats with WebP; mainly, that it's not 100% supported across all image browsers. Also, for mobile development, you typically need to include a library for it (except for Android, which supports it natively). In addition to that, the advanced nature of the lossy compression mode means that the performance of decompression on image load is a little slower than with JPG or PNG.

And Now for Choosing...

Given all these data points, there emerges a pretty clear flow diagram to decide what format to use for any given image.

1. Do you need transparency?

   - Yes → Does the client support WebP?
     - Yes → use WebP

---

5 This is how photos you take on your cellphone can be geo-tagged in your social media stream.

— No → use PNG

2. No → Does the client support WebP?

- Yes → Use WebP (unless the performance becomes a problem)
- No → Use JPG

Image Format Wars on the Internet

When it comes to the relentless bulk of web content, images are by far the largest load bearer today (although there's an argument to be made that videos have become king as of late).

But what's truly interesting is that as much as compression information can help solve some of the congestion, there's a massive amount of human problems that keep compression from making its way into everyone's hands.

Let's take a trip back to 1985, when Unisys filed a patent for the LZW compression algorithm.

A few years later, when CompuServe invented the 89a format (which later became the GIF format), they used LZW as its backbone, not realizing that it was patented. Unisys didn't care about this until 1993, when the Netscape browser added support for the IMG HTML tag, alongside support for the 89a format. Within a year, animated images became all the craze on the Internet, and Unisys began enforcing its patent. CompuServe and Unisys eventually reached a court agreement in December 1994, announcing that Unisys would begin collecting royalties from all software that used the 89a graphics format. In the months following this decision, a group of seven engineers developed an entirely new, patent-free format known as the Portable Network Graphics or PNG format. Within another few weeks, PNG was fully supported by the Netscape browser.

In 2004, the patent on LZW finally expired, but for an entire decade, the GIF/PNG image format debate was a hot one among Internet folks.[6]

JPG has been a standard for some time now, and is generally accepted by most image-editing programs and Internet browsers. In 2013, Google and a set of other open source contributors were able to create a new image codec algorithm named WebP, which aimed to compress images smaller than JPG while keeping the same image quality. WebP's savings aren't huge, maybe 5%–30%, depending on the size of the image. However, these are massive savings for companies that operate in the big image business (e.g., shopping and social sites). To these companies, a 30% reduction

---

6 With that resolved, the debate has shifted to the proper pronunciation of "GIF."

in size means a significant reduction in cost as well as faster transfer and loading times.

But there was one huge challenge with the WebP format: getting it adopted by every browser. Chrome (being developed by Google) was the first to adopt it. However, the real drama comes from the fact that the largest competitor at the time, Mozilla's Firefox, wanted nothing to do with with WebP and openly rejected it (*http://bit.ly/28NQnkB*), stating that it wasn't powerful enough (*http://muizelaar.blogspot.com/2011/04/webp.html*), and that it didn't compress as well as JPG variants (*https://mzl.la/28NQs7R*). In fact, the Mozilla engineering team even open-sourced a new MozJPEG (*https://github.com/mozilla/mozjpeg*) codec to improve the lossless preprocessor phase of JPG, all in an attempt to rebuke further WebP adoption.

This pushback didn't stop Google from implementing the codec for Google+ and its Google Play store. Facebook soon followed with support for their own implementation (*http://cnet.co/28NQuwk*), all the time praising the gains in compression and image quality. Since then, WebP adoption has been expanding, even becoming a dominant part of some compression for video games.

Mozilla's hold-out didn't last. In 2015, the company had a change of heart about the WebP format (*http://cnet.co/28MJTCG*) and stated publicly that "technology decisions often are the result of personal predilection, political scheming, and inter-company rivalries. But cold hard data still can win the day."

And there's a lot of wisdom in that statement. These stories of image formats on the Web help shed light on some interesting truths about technology adoption, programmer mentality, and customer benefit around compression. Even though an algorithm might be technically superior, it's still subject to the same product biases that relate to all types of technology output. It still must fight for acceptance and approval among a world of engineers who are generally skeptical by nature.

GPU Texture Formats

Because the computer can't draw images to the screen directly from their compressed formats, they first need to be loaded into memory and decompressed to a format that the system can use for rendering. By default, images are decompressed into 32–bits-per-pixel formats, with 8 bits going to each of the red, green, blue, and alpha channels (RGBA_8888 representations). Then the images need to be transferred to the GPU as textures, which means each bitmap you create requires CPU and GPU memory at the same time. The result of this is that regardless of the compression quality of your images on the wire, on your device these images still take up big chunks of memory.

The good news is that there exist compressed pixel formats from which the GPU can render. You take advantage of these by decompressing what comes over the wire into one of these alternate compressed formats that the GPU can render directly without a decompression step. Some of these formats are DXT (*http://bit.ly/29H7fdc*), ETC (*http://bit.ly/29H7cOl*), and PVR (*http://bit.ly/29H7hBJ*) with different profiles for lossy compression (Figure 12-7).

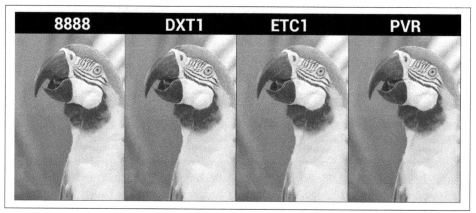

Figure 12-7. The lossy GPU formats DXT1, ETC1, and PVR are all smaller in bit-size to their RGBA_8888 counterparts, and retain high quality for many situations.

You can imagine that these compressed GPU texture formats are incredibly useful for video game developers. Not only do video games include a lot of imagery, it needs to be available in GPU memory somewhat persistently. So, any savings in memory footprint is a huge win for application smoothness and stability.

Vector Formats

Typically, images are arranged in a 2D grid of pixels, which represent the colors of the image itself. When viewed from a distance, the edging between the pixels disappears, and the human eye can see (is tricked into perceiving) smooth color gradients. This type of image is called a raster format image (*http://en.wikipedia.org/wiki/Raster_graphics*), and it can be rendered (relatively directly) to the screen.

But what if instead of sending around the final image, we send around a description of how that image was made? This is the concept behind vector image formats. Basically, these formats contain commands that when executed procedurally generate (*http://en.wikipedia.org/wiki/Procedural_generation*) a final output image.

Figure 12-8 shows the same image in raster and vector format; some trade-offs are clearly evident.

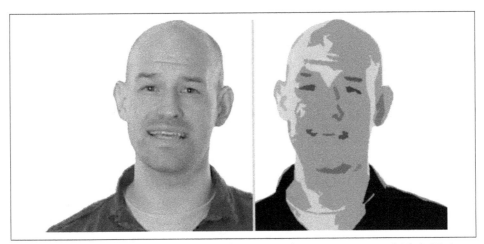

Figure 12-8. An example raster image (left) compared to a vector image (right). Notice that the vector image is much simpler and contains less per-pixel detail. This is because the format type does not lend itself to producing high-quality data.

Vector formats have some interesting benefits. For example, for some types of complex images—think technical drawings that primarily consist of lines—a list of points and how to connect them is much more efficient than sending every pixel. (It's basically a form of compression right there). Second, vector images can be scaled accurately, and that can be a huge win if you need to provide assets for thumbnails and icons and fullscreen images on a gazillion different devices.

There is a price in load time, however, because you need to create the rasterized image for the GPU by executing the commands. So, this type of format trades file size for client speed, saving bits on the wire, but incurring more client-side overhead to reconstruct the image when it's being rendered.

One commonly used vector format is SVG (*http://en.wikipedia.org/wiki/Scala ble_Vector_Graphics*). Think of SVG as a file format that makes it possible for you to store an image description at a very low memory footprint and generate a high-quality, resolution-independent image on the client, regardless of the size of the source data. One of the limitations of the SVG format is that it can represent only a certain type of image quality; that is to say that vector images tend to be simplistic, only using a set of primitive types to define how to generate colors on the screen. A field of grass in a prairie, for instance, would require too many complex shapes to yield compression savings.

Vector images are great for things like logos, technical drawings, or simple image patterns, whereas raster images are best for photos and other information-dense images.

Here is an example for your enjoyment. The following SVG produces the graphic in Figure 12-9:

```
<svg height="140" width="140">
  <defs>
    <filter id="f1" x="0" y="0" width="200%" height="200%">
      <feOffset result="offOut" in="SourceGraphic" dx="20" dy="20" />
      <feColorMatrix result = "matrixOut" in = "offOut"
        type = "matrix"
        values = "0.2 0 0 0 0 0 0.2 0 0 0 0 0 0.2 0 0 0 0 0 1 0"/>
      <feGaussianBlur result="blurOut" in="matrixOut"
        stdDeviation="10" />
      <feBlend in="SourceGraphic" in2="blurOut" mode="normal" />
    </filter>
  </defs>
  <rect width="90" height="90" stroke="green" stroke-width="3"
    fill="yellow" filter="url(#f1)" />
</svg>
```

Figure 12-9. The graphic produced by the sample SVG file.

Eyes on the Prize

For modern applications, image content makes up the bulk of data that's sent back and forth to users. Companies constantly send down thumbnails, news images, social media feeds, friend photos, and advertisements. Users, on the other hand, constantly upload pictures and content that they've created throughout their days. When you're looking at decreasing the footprint of data in your applications, images are where you should begin. It's the lowest-hanging fruit, and often small changes here can result in big wins elsewhere.

CHAPTER 13

Serialized Data

Next to image data, serialized content is the second most common data format you'll be sending around in your networked applications. And even though the lowest-hanging data compression fruit will clearly come from image data, it's equally important to take a hard look at serialized content.

What do we mean by "serialized"? Serialization is the process of taking a high-level data object and converting it to a binary string (the inverse is deserialization). This transform can be applied to a plethora of different data types, but it's most accurate when describing the conversion from an in-memory structure or class to a file or memory binary large object (BLOB) to send over a network.

This particular use case dominates the mountain of data transfers we see from modern mobile and web applications. Consider your favorite social media app. When you load it for the first time, a flurry of serialized data is passed between the client and the server in order to show you the right information on the screen. And this continues as you receive updates, news, and messages. When you post your own updated status, this input has to go into memory, be serialized to a format, uploaded to the server, which will deserialize it, add it to its database, and then serialize it again in order to send updates to all of your friends.

Although images take up the bulk of your data compression footprint by size, serialized content makes up for it in volume.

This means that performance is critical for serialization speed, deserialization speed, and the resulting file sizes that need to be sent around to millions of users. To provide some assistance here, we're going to look at the common serialized file formats XML and JSON, and discuss some techniques you can apply to make them smaller for your users.

Understanding Common Use Cases

It's important to have a clear understanding of how your serialized content is being used, because this can have a large impact on decisions you make vis-à-vis compressing that data. Here are the most common use cases.

Dynamically Server-Built Data

This is the most common type of serialized data that exists in modern mobile applications. A client object typically queries a server, perhaps asking for the results of a database operation, to which the server computes the results, serializes the content, and sends it back to the client for deserialization. In this process, the serialized data is typically compressed further by the HTTP protocol stack (for example, using GZIP), which helps to reduce the overall file size. The overhead of this decompression time on the client is well worth it, given the size savings.

Statically Built Server-Owned Data

Although dynamically built data is common, applications typically use static serialized content as well; for example, sending the client configuration files for the latest build. The author can update these files on the server on a semiregular basis, and that's usually done offline. As such, the server simply views these files as static and passes them off to the client upon request. Again, these files tend to be further compressed by the HTTP stack.

Dynamically Client-Built Data

In many situations, the client will send information to some server, in which case the creation of this serialized information occurs on the client. This means that the overhead for performing serialization and the data compression process reside entirely on the client device. For laptops or desktops, this might not be an issue, but for mobile phones, tablets, and wearable devices, this can spell big trouble over time. In addition, because those devices tend to be lower powered, there's typically less of a desire to spend client resources on hyper-compressing data further for upload. This creates a unique balancing act that developers will need to work out for their specific applications

Statically Client-Owned Data

Finally, there is data that resides on and is used locally by the client; for example, layout information that's authored once and then loaded many times without further changes. This information is quite easy to compress, typically during the build-time of an application, while extra machine power is available. The only thing the client needs to do is keep the data resident (on persistent storage) and load its content into memory on demand.

Issues with Serialized Formats

The two biggest serialization formats used today are JSON (*http://www.json.org/*) and XML (*https://en.wikipedia.org/wiki/XML*). This is mostly due to their adoption by the web platform over the past 20 years. Although easy to use, and hugely popular, these formats present some very specific compression issues.

Human-Readable Text

One of the draws of JSON and XML is that they are (more or less) human readable. That is, if you opened the post-serialized file in your text editor, you'd be able to read the entire thing, as demonstrated in this random JSON snippet:

```
{
  "base": {
    "reboot": { ...omitted for brevity... },
    "updateBaseConfiguration": { ...omitted for brevity... }
  },
  "robot": {
    "jump": {
      "parameters": {
        "height": {
          "type": "integer",
          "minimum": 0,
          "maximum": 100
        },
        "_jumpType": {
          "type": "string",
          "enum": [ "_withAirFlip", "_withSpin", "_withKick" ]
        }
      }
    },
    "speak": {
      "parameters": {
        "phrase": {
          "type": "string",
          "enum": [ "beamMeUpScotty", "iDontDigOnSwine", "iPityDaFool",
                    "dangerWillRobinson" ]
        },
        "volume": {
          "type": "integer",
          "minimum": 0,
          "maximum": 10
        }
      }
    }
  }
}
```

```
        }
    }
```

As you can see, this is done by representing the entire file as a set of string values, cobbled together by tokens, to define how everything is related.

The benefit is an amazingly flexible format (almost any data structure can find a way to be properly serialized to these formats), but the downside is a massive amount of overhead in order to include all that human-readable information.

Looking at the preceding JSON snippet, a large number of spaces, line breaks, and string quotes are included, simply to make this file more human readable. As a result, the encoded file is larger, in bits, than it needs to be. The problem becomes worse with numerical data. For example, if your serialized JSON file contains the string "3.141592653589793", it would be 17 bytes long (or even longer, depending on your character encoding). This is completely insane, considering that the actual floating-point number used to represent this number is only 8 bytes (or 64 bits) long. The human-readable version is more than twice the size of the binary one.

Slow Decode Times

It's important to note that decode times can often be problematic for these text formats. The reason for this is multifold:

- String-based input must be converted to memory objects using heavy-handed operations (for example, converting ASCII symbols to integer numbers is not cheap).
- Holding data in temporary memory during load time isn't always efficient.
- Backward compatibility to older formats can slow encoding and decoding.

The takeaway is that formats like XML and JSON, by default, skew toward longer load times in order to properly deserialize on the client. In fact, there's an array of XML and JSON encoders out there that are entirely focused on reducing load times for specifically organized file types.

Smaller Serialized Data

With all of this in mind, there's a few tricks you can employ to help reduce the size of JSON and XML data as it's being sent to your users.

Use a Binary Serialization Format

Easily, the biggest bang for the buck is kicking JSON and XML to the curb, and finding a binary serialization format to go with instead. Binary formats lack the human-readable nature of JSON and XML, but they ensure that the data is encoded in a compact and efficient binary form. The results are smaller files and faster load times.

Even though binary serialization formats are in abundance, some of our favorites lie in the middle ground between wire-size format and decompression time. If you're willing to define your own schema Protobufs (*https://developers.google.com/protocol-buffers/*), Flatbuffers (*https://google.github.io/flatbuffers/*), or Cap'n Proto (*https://capn proto.org*) should be the first formats you evaluate for these benefits.

But suppose that you are not ready to abandon the XML or JSON ship, or your boss won't let you get off the text-based serialization wagon. There are ways in which you can improve your JSON data to serialize it more efficiently and also make it more compressible. Formats such as BSON (*http://bsonspec.org*) and MSGPACK (*http://msgpack.org*) keep the correct JSON schema but provide binary sizes for encoding. This would let you get better file size but not have to lift so much of your code to do so.

The real joy of these binary formats is that they produce better compression than their human-readable counterparts, and in some cases, they can actually be compressed further by general-purpose encoders such as GZIP.

Restructure Lists for Better Compression

Here's an interesting point. When you're serializing your data, most of the time, you're doing so to mirror the in-memory object form of the content. Looking at the next code snippet, consider the structure on the left, and how it's serialized to JSON on the right.

```
struct {                     {
    int id;                      "id": 25,
    char* name;                  "name": "Hooty McOwlface",
    int gender;                  "gender": 27,
    int age;                     "age": 88,
    char* address;               "address": "1600 Amphitheatre Pkwy, Mountain View, CA 94043"
    int employeeID;              "employeeID": 3025
}                            },
```

The ordering of attributes in the JSON file tends to follow the in-memory representation of the corresponding structure. Although this is fine for ease of programmer maintenance, it doesn't produce the best compression results after you get an entire list of structures.

First, consider that a JSON object (picking on JSON for a minute) is made up of key-value pairs (*http://bit.ly/29H72Xz*), where the key portion is repeated for each instance of the structure in the file, adding bloat. In the following list of people and their countries, you need to repeat the "name" and "country" keywords for every single person:

```
...
{
    "name": "Joanna",
    "country": "USA"
}{
    "name": "Alex",
    "country": "AUS"
},
{
    "name": "Colt",
    "country": "USA"
}
...
```

For large JSON files that list many elements in this form, the amount of overhead per each occurrence of "name" and "country" contributes a great deal to the final byte size.

Second, recall that encoders like GZIP and its brethren are all based on the LZ algorithm for their primary transform step, meaning that they are most powerful when they can find repeated data patterns in their search window.

Imagine an entire file of such employee data and realize that there are gaps between values that are potential duplicates. For example, the "age" value might be further than the 1 K to 2 K search window away from the next "age" value in the serialized file.

You can address both repetition of keys and distance of similar values by a simple reordering of the list content. You can transpose the previous array structure[1] such that all the values for a given key are held in a single array and close together, as demonstrated in the following example:[2]

```
{
    "name": ["Joanna", "Alex", "Colt"],
    "country": ["USA", "AUS", "USA"]
}
```

This reduces bloat and makes it easier for the LZ algorithm to find matches.

In programming-speak, the truth is that converting from array-of-structs to struct-of-arrays can be a critically important transform for large serialized content. So, if you're dealing with big JSON or XML files, seriously consider this type of transform.

---

1 Which, technically is called "array of structs" or rather, "a list of data objects."

2 It's worth pointing out that this is not a concept unique to serialized content. If you've ever had to deal with runtime performance relating to a CPUs L2 Cache residency (*https://goo.gl/2HSyOJ*), the solution is the same.

Organize for Efficient Fetching

We can extend the concept of transposing structures a bit further. Do you really need to fetch fully structured data from the server? Or could you instead request each data type separately (and assemble them in the client, if necessary)?

There is a tendency for backend applications to provide a general-purpose API for all of their clients. Although this is a reasonable strategy for backend systems, it's not good for the client, because the application ends up transferring and processing a lot of data on a small device when some calculations could be made more efficiently on the server farms.

If your application displays a feed of mixed content, ensure that the client can fetch that information in a single request and that the returned data is suitable for caching in pieces. You generally want your client to be able to identify entities so that it can store them persistently, and also avoid duplicates of the same objects in memory.

While doing this type of data fetching, many APIs return hierarchical data where all relations are denormalized. Although this is the preferred approach for most web clients, it is not good for mobile clients for which persisting data and serving it from local storage is important.

Instead of returning hierarchical data, it is better to return normalized data.

Take a look at the following bad example. The same user_id and user_name is duplicated in many places. The client will need to decompose this one big object, extract nested user objects, get rid of duplicates, and store what's left in the local database or memory cache.

```
{
"messages" : [{
    "from" : {
            "user_id" : 1,
            "user_name" : "claude",
            ....
        },
        "text" : "hello
hello",
        "date" : "123"
},
{
    "from" : {
    "user_id" : 1,
    "user_name" : "claude",
    ....
},
"text" : "how are you",
"date" : "124"
},
{
```

```
        "from" : {
        "user_id" : 1,
        "user_name" : "claude",
        ....
    },
    "text" : "you there",
    "date" : "125"
    },
    {
        "from" : {
        "user_id" : 1,
        "user_name" : "claude",
        ....
    },
    "text" : "hello
hello",
    "date" : "126"
    }]
}
```

Now look at this better example:

```
{
"users" : {
        "1" : {
    "user_id" : 1,
    "user_name" : "claude",
    ....
        }
},
"messages" : [{
    "from" : 1,
        "text" : "hello
hello",
        "date" : "123"
    },
    {
        "from" : 1,
    "text" : "how are you",
    "date" : "124"
    },
    {
        "from" : 1,
    "text" : "you there",
    "date" : "125"
    },
    {
        "from" : 1,
    "text" : "hello
hello",
    "date" : "126"
    }]
}
```

This is much easier for the client because each object is passed only once. The returned "users" hash in the response can easily be used to update the database and in-memory cache.

But we can do even better and completely flatten our hierarchy. Check out this final solution. It's all the same information, without duplication; compact, and straightforward to process.

```
                {
    "users" : {
            "1" : {
        "user_id" : 1,
        "user_name" : "claude",
        ....
            }
    },
    "messages" : {
    "from": [1,1,1,1],
    "text": [ "hello
    hello","how are you","you there","hello
    hello"],
    }
```

The more information the client has about the data it is displaying, the more efficient it can be. The application can decide which data to cache or prune and, for example, how to invalidate the layout when new data arrives. A mobile client is a lot more sophisticated than a simple HTML renderer, and you give it due respect by handing it the best possible structured data.

Segment Out Data into the Proper Compression Format

Typically these types of serialized formats, such as JSON and XML, are "junk drawers" for multiple types of data. You can combine integers, strings, floats, even images and sound data, all encoded right into the silly little serialized format.

However, separating out these large data types into their own compressed chunks will yield better compression than letting them be in-line in the file. Think about it. If you have a JSON file with 2,600 inverted indexes, GZIP isn't going to help you much. However, separating out the indexes, and delta-compressing them first, can yield significant improvements.

It goes likewise for images. There was a scary trend for a while to base64-encode (*https://en.wikipedia.org/wiki/Base64*) PNG files (that is, to represent the binary data in an ASCII string format) inside of CSS files for doing responsive web design. The use case made sense: It costs more "load time" to make the extra network transfer for the thumbnail than the overhead from transferring the bloated image content inside the CSS file. We don't condone this action for mobile applications, except in rare cases (*http://www.mobify.com/blog/data-uris-are-slow-on-mobile/*).

When you are busy figuring out how to create that moment of utter delight for your users, thinking about data compression is probably not at the forefront of your mind. We would like to argue that it should be, at least for a few moments every day. Like with every other bit of app infrastructure, building it into your app development process ultimately takes less work for better results. That will translate pretty directly into happier users, and perhaps, a sweeter bottom line.

Whether you are going to use built-in compressors or no compression at all, or a customized pipeline for each type of data, the important thing is that you make your choices consciously, and based on as much data as you can get your hands on.

Building a strong pipeline for image compression and data serialization can help support your application through its lifetime. Starting with the right mentality for data compression in your development helps keep things slim and thin for your users as you carry on. So do this in the beginning, rather than at the end...OK?

CHAPTER 14

Lossy Data Compression

You've probably noticed that this book has spent a *lot* of time dealing with algorithms that are *lossless* in nature. That is, the decoded version of the data is bit-identical to the source version of the data.

However, most of the content you're really worried about in the day-to-day operation of your application is compressed by *lossy* compressors. Things like images, sounds, and video contain far more information than the human visual and audio systems can process—or need—to fully enjoy the experience. Lossy compression formats get rid of those extra bits.

Lossy compressors are typically applied to the data first, to reduce its dynamic range, in preparation for further lossless compression.

Let's be clear about this: there is an unlimited number of lossy compressors out there, depending on your data type, needs, and how much error your users are willing to tolerate. In reality, it's one of the most fertile grounds for data compression science because there's just so much left undone there.

So, why didn't we talk more about lossy compression algorithms in this book?

Because...well...that's a different book.

CHAPTER 15

Making the World a Little Smaller

Data Compression and You

So, we've finally reached the end of this book, which details algorithms that began in the 1960s and have had a clear and pronounced influence on computing and technology to the present time. But where are things going from here? Many engineers will happily throw up their hands and say that compression is a solved problem, or that it is not significant to their skill set. The truth is that over the next few decades, data compression will remain as important as it was back then. So, it's perhaps worthwhile to take a look at how interconnected data compression is with you, your company, and the future of technology.

Data Compression and the Bottom Line

When it comes down to you and your company, it's all about the money. Hard, cold, fast cash. Data compression is so interwoven to your bottom line that companies who can get this part of their tech stack right save when it comes to the following things:

- User acquisition and retention
- Running costs
- Planning ahead

Let's dig in a bit.

User Acquisition and Retention

There is a direct relationship between how fast web pages load and conversion rates. If pages don't load fast enough, users will abandon whatever they are doing, including buying your products. On the other hand, the slimmer the data you pack into your product page, the faster it will load, and the more likely users will buy and return in the future.

The average statistics show that one in four users will abandon a mobile page load that takes longer than four seconds. It's worth testing your pages, because this could mean massive impact on the bottom line, just from page loads. If you need convincing, here are some real-life stories:

- Amazon has shown that for every 100 milliseconds of slowdown (*http://bit.ly/29H7qFb*), it experienced a 1% drop in revenue. Or, to take a different turn on stats, a giant, such as Amazon, would suffer an annual loss of $1.6 billion (*http://bit.ly/29H7oNL*) if its pages loaded just 1 second slower. On the other hand, Amazon increased revenue by 1% for every 100 milliseconds of improved page load speed.
- Walmart's latest reports show that for every 1 second of page load improvement, it experienced up to a 2% increase in conversions (*http://www.slideshare.net/devonauerswald/walmart-pagespeedslide*). For every 100 milliseconds of improvement, it grew incremental revenue by up to 1%.
- Shopzilla sped up its average page load time from 6 seconds to 1.2 seconds and increased revenue by 12%, as well as page views by 25%.
- Small sites, such as AutoAnything, cut their load time in half and saw revenue grow by 13% (*https://en.wikipedia.org/wiki/AutoAnything*).
- President Obama's 2012 presidential campaign based its entire fundraising success on making its website load instantly (*http://bit.ly/29H7lBr*).

In addition, better site reviews, more word-of-mouth downloads, and better retention can probably save your marketing departments lots of money.

Running Costs

The content of your websites has to be stored somewhere, and that somewhere is usually a bunch of hard drives in a big fat cloud. Hard drives cost money. Shipping data to and from the cloud costs money. Renting (or building and running) data center space and bandwidth costs money. And even though cloud technology is normalizing and costs are coming down significantly, bandwidth and storage remain challenging financial problems for big companies.

In 2015, Netflix (*http://nflx.it/29H7FQD*) announced that it was going to begin modifying the compression technology for its video streams; adjusting which algorithm was used on what video depending on the noisiness of the content itself. This move was projected to save the company massive amounts in terms of bandwidth costs, and allowed it to accommodate to the performance of specific devices.

Also in 2015, Facebook (*http://bit.ly/28L1JBD*)published details on how it serves preview images, which are only 200 bytes each. Considering how many images the social media network sends around on a daily basis, this was a huge win for them, especially for users on 2G devices.

You don't need an advanced degree in mathematics to understand this one: smaller data results in smaller outbound costs, less inbound costs, and fewer storage costs.

Planning Ahead

Web pages are getting bigger. An independent website, HTTPArchive (*http://httparch ive.org*), has been downloading, cataloging, and gathering statistics on the top 1,000 web pages since about 2011. One of the interesting stats gathered during analysis is the average size of these websites. This statistic sums the bytes required to display the page information, including JavaScript, HTML, CSS, JPG, and video. This page size reportedly grew by 24% in 2013 (*http://bit.ly/28L1JBL*), landing at about 1.5 MB per page, and in 2015, it hit 2 MB in size (*http://bit.ly/29H7816*).

One reason why websites are growing larger is because they contain more images, and those images are increasing in size. In addition, there is more code as websites are becoming more complex overall. This problem is becoming so bad for users on 2G, that big companies like Google launched a new framework called Accelerated Mobile Pages (*http://bit.ly/28L1IxD*), which specifically targets sites to reduce their dependency graph, image sizes, and basically tries to offer leaner, faster content to users on bad bandwidth.

Making Your Users' Lives a Little More Magical and Less Expensive

Mobile devices make up a surprisingly important part of modern life. It's madness to think that the user experience of that hinges so critically on how fast pictures of cats can be streamed from a server to a phone.

And while you're trying to cut costs for outbound data, users are trying to do the same for inbound data. Let's be clear here: users pay for everything. And most of them pay for data, by the megabyte, and at outrageous rates.

mobiForge did a nice little analysis in 2013 (*http://bit.ly/28L2734*) that showed the costs for connecting to data on high-tariff data plans. At that time, AT&T's roaming rates charged $12 per megabyte. Users who browsed to *microsoft.com* ended up paying AT&T $17.50 each time.

But it's not just the money cost. Consider battery overhead as well. Users who are on slower connections take longer to download content, which means that their battery is on longer for the same piece of content than on a faster connection. The result is that users on slower connections drain batteries faster.

Data compression is directly related to all these issues. Smaller assets means less time to download on worse connections, and less battery drain. The end result? Faster cat pictures to your users.

Thinking About What's Next in Technology

If you're lucky enough to live in a country with amazingly well-adopted connectivity, congrats to you! Chances are you're paying pretty sane rates for a pretty good mobile connection. Worldwide, however, this isn't the case. More humans on the planet have bad connections than good ones. Looking forward, the future of mobile computing is going to be defined by the next five billion humans who are about to jump online for the first time, and the quality of their mobile networks.

The Next Five Billion Users

There are 7.4 billion humans on the planet right now (*http://www.worldometers.info/world-population/*). About 2 billion of them are currently connected to the Internet. Most of the rest live in countries that are rapidly expanding their connectivity. This means that your largest growth potential is in the emerging markets of Asia and Africa. The advancement in mobile computing technology over the last decade means that the next billion humans will be coming online, for the first time, from a mobile phone rather than a desktop or laptop device.

In their book, *New Digital Age* (Penguin Random House), authors Eric Schmidt and Jared Cohen lay out the topic well:

> There are already more than 650 million mobile phone users in Africa, and close to 3 billion across Asia. The majority of these people are using basic-feature phones—voice calls and text messages only—because the cost of data service in their countries is often prohibitively expensive, so that even those who can buy web-enabled phones or smartphones cannot use them affordably. This will change, and when it does, the smartphone revolution will profoundly benefit these populations.

Mobile Networks

Building networks for these high-saturation-potential countries will not be cheap. If you consider that Verizon had to shell out $50 billion (*http://cnnmon.ie/28L2z1a*) to simply upgrade its network to 4G, the cost of building an entirely new network for such a massive population must be astronomical. Such costs will often be inflated due to government entanglement (as is common for government and telecom companies), and this generally will result in passing off all costs to the end customer.

The world has been seeing great improvement in network speeds over the past few years. However, it's important to see how this improvement is not uniform in terms of numbers, or geolocation. Google Analytics has a set of fantastic charts (*http://analyt ics.blogspot.com/2013/04/is-web-getting-faster.html*) showing the trends in connectivity, worldwide. It's easy to see that the idea of improvement is not homogeneous. For instance, China saw an 8% *increase* in median page load time for desktop computers (things got slower), whereas their mobile performance time *decreased 33%* (things got faster), but still landing at >3.5 seconds load time. This is a pretty big number, *considering 42% of their 1.53 billion population is online.*

The short form is this: mobile networks will continue to grind their way to increase speed, (*http://en.wikipedia.org/wiki/LTE_(telecommunication)*) slowly, unevenly, and at great expense. If you're waiting for the mobile web to suddenly get faster, you might need to find a more comfortable chair to wait around in.

For example, a 2G network has ~0.021 MB/sec transfer speed, whereas GZIP can compress 61 MB/sec. Even a reduction of 10 times in GZIP speed would still access a single megabyte faster than the network could transfer it. Colt's analysis of these data points suggests that *it would be cheaper to invest in a better compressing-slower decompression codec than it would be to invest millions of dollars upgrading the network hardware.*

...Starting Now

The picture painted here should be immediately clear. The next great computing revolution will come from areas of massive populations that tend to be skewed toward the entry-level economic ladder, meaning that their choices in mobile hardware and cell provider will be skewed toward slower hardware and slower networks.

But there will be the same demand for fast data, and there will be the same competition between developers for the attention of those users. The trends in mobile computing continue, and average app data costs continue to skyrocket; however, these individuals are playing a catch-up game in which they are already far behind. The user cost to send down 25 thumbnails or load a page of news headlines with images might be too much and too slow for these users, causing them to abandon slow experiences for much faster ones.

This problem is so important in 2015 that even large developers like Facebook have rolled out slimmed down, 2G-friendly versions (*https://www.facebook.com/lite/*) of their experience, just to reduce barriers for acquiring users in this budding mobile market.

And as a developer, you can't really control the networks, and you can't control the hardware. But you can control the data, and with that, you can do a great amount to ensure that it is compressed aggressively so that it arrives to users with a speed and quality that lets them have a valid computing experience and remain faithful to your application over time.

What are you waiting for?

Glossary of Compression Words

7zip (*http://www.7-zip.org*)

A file archiver with a high compression ratio.

Alpha blending

The process of combining an image with a background to create the appearance of partial or full transparency.

Alpha channel

An additional channel (in addition to RGB) that contains a value between 0 and 1 that designates the transparency for each pixel.

Alpha transparency

The transparency value for a pixel as transmitted in the Alpha channel.

Arithmetic coding

An algorithm for encoding data, wherein frequently used characters are stored with fewer bits and not-so-frequently occurring characters are stored with more bits, resulting in fewer bits used in total. Rather than assigning codewords to symbols in a 1:1 fashion, this algorithm transforms the entire input stream from a set of symbols to one (excessively long) numeric value, whose LOG2 representation is closer to the true value of entropy for the stream.

See Chapter 5.

Asymmetric numeral systems (ANS) (*http://arxiv.org/abs/1311.2540*)

A modern variant of statistical compression, which has shown early promise in achieving close to entropy compression with performance comparable to *Huffman coding*.

See Chapter 5.

Binary or base 2 number system

A way of representing numbers using only the digits 0 and 1, and each shift in position is by a power of 2. For example, the decimal number 5 would be 101 or $2^0 + 2^2$.

See Chapter 2.

Binary erasure channel

A communications channel model used for analysis in *information theory*. The idea is that a bit is never wrong. It either exists and is correct or it is "erased."

Binary search

An algorithm for finding a target value in a sorted array.

Bitwise exclusive OR (XOR)

bitwise = operates on each bit independently

exclusive OR (XOR) = a logical operation that outputs TRUE only when both inputs differ (one is TRUE, the other is FALSE).

Block codes

Any error-correcting code that encodes data in blocks.

Blocking

The act of subdividing a set of data into smaller "blocks" for the purpose of better compression.

Block sorting compression

The name for a performant application of the *Burrows–Wheeler transform*, which will block separate the data stream, and apply *BWT* to each block, rather than the entire stream.

BMP file

A file format for bitmaps (simple raster, encoded images with RGB channels).

BSON (*http://bsonspec.org*)

A binary version of the *JSON* serialization format.

Burrows–Wheeler transform (BWT), block-sorting compression

Example of a reversible transform that rearranges a character string into runs of similar characters.

See Chapter 8.

BZIP/BZIP2

Free and open source file compression program that uses the *Burrows–Wheeler transform* to compress single files.

Bytecode

Instruction set made up of compact numeric codes designed for efficient execution by a software interpreter.

Cap'n Proto (*https://capnproto.org*)

A binary serialization format.

Channel

The means by which information is transmitted.

Claude Shannon

An American mathematician, known as the "father of information theory." He is also the reason why this book exists. So,

read this Wikipedia article to find out what a mess he got us into.

Coder

See *encoder*.

Codec

Short for *coder-decoder*. A device or computer program capable of encoding or decoding a digital data stream or signal.

Coding theory

Science of finding explicit methods, called codes, for increasing the efficiency and reducing the error rate of data communication over noisy channels to near the channel capacity. These codes can be roughly subdivided into data compression (source coding) and error-correction (channel coding) techniques. A third class of information theory codes are cryptographic algorithms.

Communication

The purposeful activity of information exchange between two or more participants in order to convey or receive the intended meanings through a shared system of signs and semiotic rules. The fundamental problem of communication is that of reproducing at one point, either exactly or approximately, a message selected at another point.

Context modeling

The process of using multiple information signals about a piece of data to infer what the best type of compression algorithm is to apply to it.

Contextual compressor

Compressor that determines the output symbol based on the probability of the input symbol in the current context.

See Chapter 8.

Convolutional code

A type of error-correction code used to increase the reliability of data transfers.

Cryptographic algorithms

Algorithms to encode information with the purpose of making transmission more secure: keeping the content secret.

Data compression

Representing the information in a data stream with fewer bits than the original stream. For example, writing "Rolling on the floor laughing" as "ROFL" compresses the original from 29 to 4 characters, which is a savings of 86%. (This also hints at the fact that having context can increase compression rate.)

Data stream

A block of data that's intended to be consumed in small groups at a time rather than having access to every part of the stream at once. A real-life example is listening to music on a radio.

Decoder

Part of compression software that is responsible for translating the compressed stream back into uncompressed data.

DEFLATE

A popular compression algorithm that utilizes *LZ* and *statistical encoding* to achieve compression.

Dictionary encoding

The process of transforming your data stream based upon most common symbol groupings.

See Chapter 7.

Dynamic range of data set

For the purpose of this book, the number of bits needed to represent every value in the data.

Encoder

Part of compression software that is responsible for translating the source information into compressed data form.

Entropy

See *information entropy*.

Error-correcting code

A code attached to a chunk of information that can be as simple as confirmation that the information is correct, or complex enough to "fix" errors.

Error correction

Attaching a code to a chunk of information that makes it possible to detect and correct errors in transmitted data. Error detection and correction codes increase the reliability of information and make it more resilient to noise. Error correction is orthogonal to compression.

Finite state entropy (FSE) (*https://github.com/Cyan4973/FiniteStateEntropy*)

A practical implementation of *asymmetric numeral systems*, which is focused more dominantly on improved performance.

Flatbuffers (*https://google.github.io/flatbuffers/*)

An efficient open source cross-platform serialization library originally created at Google for game development and other performance-critical applications.

Grouping

In the context of compression, assigning bits to a group of symbols instead of to individual symbols. For example, in text, you could encode the 100 most common words. Finding out which strings/substrings to group is its own challenge.

GIF

An image compression format known for its Alpha transparency support and animated image usage.

gzip (GNU zip) (*http://www.gzip.org/#intro*)

Unpatented compression utility widely used on the Internet.

H.264

Video coding format that is currently one of the most commonly used formats for the recording, compression, and distribution of video content. H.264 is perhaps best known as being one of the video encoding standards for Blu-ray discs and video streaming. The format is patented.

H.264 is typically used for lossy data compression in the strict mathematical sense, although the amount of loss can sometimes be imperceptible. It is also possible to create truly lossless data compression using it—e.g., to have localized lossless-coded regions within lossy-coded pictures, or to support rare use cases for which the entire encoding is lossless.

Histogram

A diagram consisting of rectangles whose area is proportional to the frequency of a variable, and whose width is equal to the class interval.

HTTP protocol stack

The suite of protocols that make up the HyperText Transport Protocol (HTTP).

Huffman coding

Prefix-based lossless data compression encoding.

See Chapter 5.

Information

For our purposes, the content of a message. Information can be encoded into various forms for transmission and interpretation (for example, information can be encoded into a sequence of symbols or transmitted via a sequence of signals).

Information resolves uncertainty. The uncertainty of an event is measured by its probability of occurrence and is inversely proportional to that. The more uncertain an event, the more information is required to resolve uncertainty of that event.

Information content

The actual information contained in a datastream (versus *noise*). See also information entropy.

Information entropy

The average number of bits needed to store or communicate one symbol in a message.

See Chapter 3.

Information theory

The branch of mathematics, electrical engineering, and computer science involving quantification of information. Information theory studies the transmission, processing, utilization, and extraction of information.

ITU

Short for International Telecommunication Union.

JPG/JPEG

Lossy data compression format widely used for digital images.

JSON format

JavaScript Object Notation (JSON) is a data-interchange format that in addition to being easy for machines to parse and generate, is easy for humans to read and write.

Key-value pairs

Representing data as collection of pairs—for example, [word, definition] or [row, value].

Laplace estimator

A formula used to estimate underlying probabilities when there are few observations, or for events that have not been observed to occur at all in (finite) sample data.

Lempel–Ziv and Lempel–Ziv–Welch algorithms

A family of lossless algorithms for tokenizing data streams.

See Chapter 7.

Least significant bit (LSB)

The bit in a binary number that has the smallest numerical value.

For example, in the binary number 1000, the LSB is the right-most digit with the value 0.

Lexicographic order

A generalization of the way the alphabetical order of words is based on the alphabetical order of their component letters.

Lexicographic permutation

Clustering groups of the same symbol near each other. See also *BWT*.

List decoding

The main idea behind list decoding is that the decoding algorithm, instead of outputting a single possible message, outputs a list of possibilities, one of which is correct. This allows for handling a greater number of errors than that allowed by unique decoding.

Linear correlation

A relationship or connection between two things based on co-occurrence or pattern of change, where if one of them changes, the other one changes linearly. For example: if the temperature increases, ice cream sales also increase. Most important: correlation does not imply causation.

Literal stream

A data stream that only holds literal (unencoded) values for symbols.

See Chapter 6.

Literal token

An output token that indicates that the next symbol should be read/written from/to the *literal stream*.

See Chapter 6.

Lossless data compression

Applying compression techniques where no information is lost during compression, and the original information can be fully and exactly reconstructed.

Logic synthesis

In electronics, a process by which an abstract form of desired circuit behavior is turned into a design implementation in terms of logic gates.

Lossy data compression

Refers to compression techniques wherein some information is lost during compression, and the original information cannot be fully and exactly reconstructed. The goal of lossy compression is to find a bal-ance between maximum compression and sufficient fidelity to the original data.

LZA (*http://encode.ru/threads/1969-LZA-archiver*)

Archiver based on the *LZ77* algorithm.

LZMA

Archiver based on the *LZ77* algorithm.

LZ77, LZ78

A family of algorithms that achieves compression by replacing repeated occurrences of data with references to a single copy of that data existing earlier in the uncompressed data stream. Other implementations include LZFSE (download) (*http://apple.co/28MjogJ*), LZHAM (*https://github.com/richgel999/lzham_codec*), and LZTurbo (*https://sites.google.com/site/powturbo/*).

Locality-dependent skewing

We totally made this term up, and what we mean by it is skewing that is different at different locations of the data stream.

Markov chain

Named after Andrey Markov, a random process that undergoes transitions from one state to another on a state space. It must possess a property that is usually characterized as "memorylessness": the probability distribution of the next state depends only on the current state and not on the sequence of events that preceded it.

Mathematical origami

The mathematical study of origami.

Most significant bit (MSB)

The bit in a binary number that has the highest numerical value. In the binary number 1000, the MSB on the left-most side of the number has a value 8.

Move-to-front (MTF)

A data transformation algorithm that is locally adaptive.

See Chapter 8.

MSGPACK (*http://msgpack.org*)

Small and fast binary serializaton format.

Mumbo jumbo (*https://goo.gl/gAqC02*)

What's inside Fibonacci encodings.

Multicontext coders

Algorithms that weave together multiple symbols and statistical tables or models in order to identify the least number of bits needed to encode the next symbol.

See Chapter 9.

Multiset

A set where multiple occurrences of the same element are considered.

Mutual information

A measure of information that is in common between two random variables.

n-grams

A contiguous sequence of n items from a given sequence of text or speech.

Noise

Anything that corrupts a signal or information between the source and the recipient.

Nonsingular codes

A code is nonsingular if each source symbol is mapped to a different non-empty bit string.

Normalization

Adjusting values measured on different scales to a notionally common scale.

Permutation

In mathematics, the notion of permutation relates to the act of rearranging, or permuting, all the members of a set into some sequence or order.

Prediction by Partial Matching (PPM)

An algorithm based on Markov chains with many variants, including PPM*, PPMD, and PPMZ.

See Chapter 9.

Prefix code

A code is a prefix code if no target bit string in the mapping is a prefix of the target bit string of a different source symbol

in the same mapping. This means that symbols can be decoded instantaneously after their entire codeword is received. Prefix codes are always *nonsingular* and *uniquely decodable*.

Prefix property

This property prescribes that after a code has been assigned to a symbol, no other code can start with that bit pattern. A required property for *variable-length codes*.

Probability distribution

A statistical function that describes all the possible values and likelihoods that a random variable can take within a given range. This range will be between the minimum and maximum statistically possible values, but where the possible value is likely to be plotted on the probability distribution depends on a number of factors, including the distributions mean, standard deviation, and *skewness* (*http://www.investopedia.com/terms/s/skewness.asp*).

Program synthesis

Automatically generating a program that satisfies a set of requirements.

Protocol buffers, protobuffs (*https://developers.google.com/protocol-buffers/*)

Google's language-neutral, platform-neutral, extensible mechanism for serializing structured data.

Quantization

The procedure of constraining something from a continuous set of values (such as the real numbers) to a relatively small discrete set (such as the integers).

Quantification

The act of counting and measuring that maps human sense observations and experiences into members of some set of numbers. For example, expressing the level of noise at a concert in decibels.

Qbit, qubit

Short for quantum bit. The basic unit of information in a quantum computer. Also used to designate a very, very small amount of something.

Rate

The average entropy per symbol.

Range coding

An algorithm that does basically the same as arithmetic coding but is free of patents.

Redundancy

Words or data that could be omitted without loss of meaning or function; repetition or superfluity of information. For example, in "there were ten (10) ducks in the pond," "(10)" is redundant.

In information theory, the number of bits used to transmit a message minus the number of bits of actual information in the message.

Run-length encoding (RLE)

RLE takes advantage of the adjacent clustering of symbols that occur in succession. It replaces a "run" of symbols with a tuple containing the symbol and the number of times it is repeated.

See Chapter 8.

Serialization

The process of converting objects or data structures into strings of bits that can be stored or transmitted. It is implied that the original object can be reconstructed using deserialization.

Shannon–Fano coding

Technique for constructing a *prefix code* based on a set of symbols and their probabilities (estimated or measured). It is suboptimal in the sense that it does not achieve the lowest possible expected codeword length like *Huffman coding*; however, unlike Huffman coding, it does guarantee that all codeword lengths are within one bit of their theoretical ideal.

Sources

Objects that encode message data and transmit the information, via a channel, to one or more receivers. Any process that generates successive messages. Also called the "sender."

Statistical compression

Compression that determines the output symbol based on the probability of the input symbol.

See Chapter 5.

Statistical skewing

In probability theory and statistics, skewness is a measure of the asymmetry of the probability distribution of a real-valued random variable about its mean. Or in plain language, a measure for how much more probable some symbols are than others. For example, the English alphabet is skewed in that the letter "e" is a lot more common than the letter "q". For compression, skewing is a good thing, and some data transforms manipulate the set of symbols to increase skewing.

tANS

A variant of ANS or arithmetic numerical systems described in Jarek Duda's paper "Asymmetric Numeral Systems: Entropy Coding Combining Speed of Huffman Coding with Compression Rate of Arithmetic Coding" (*http://arxiv.org/abs/1311.2540*).

See Chapter 5.

Tokenizing a stream

Assigning symbols to the contents of a stream. For example, in lexical analysis, tokenization is the process of breaking a stream of text into words, phrases, symbols, or other meaningful elements called tokens. In the context of compression, it's about finding best way of assigning a dictionary of "words" to a stream.

Transformation of data

In the context of compression, making changes to a data stream (without changing the information content) to make it more compressible. For example, in [123456,123457,123458], the delta from number N to number N + 1 might require fewer bits than N + 1, such as [123456,1,1]. Finding the right transformation for a given datastream is in itself a big challenge.

Trie

In computer science, a trie, also called "digital tree" and sometimes "radix tree" or "prefix tree" (as they can be searched by prefixes), is an ordered tree data structure that is used to store a dynamic set or associative array where the keys are usually strings.

Unary encoding

An entropy encoding that represents a natural number, n, with n ones followed by a zero (if *natural number* is understood as *non-negative integer*) or with $n-1$ ones followed by a zero (if *natural number* is understood as *strictly positive integer*). For example, 5 is represented as 111110 or 11110. The ones and zeros are interchangeable.

Unicode

Unicode is a computing industry standard for the consistent encoding, representation, and handling of text expressed in most of the world's writing systems. The latest version of Unicode contains a repertoire of more than 120,000 characters covering 129 modern and historic scripts, as well as multiple symbol sets.

Uniquely decodable codes

A code is uniquely decodable if its extension is nonsingular—which means that the target symbols are uniquely identifiable.

Universal code

A way of creating variable-length codes for positive integers by mapping each integer to a unique binary encoding. In general, the smallest integers are assigned the fewest bits.

Variable-length codes or VLC

Codes that use encodings that vary in length. Usually the shortest encodings are applied to the most common symbols in the data set.

See Chapter 4.

Video codec

An electronic circuit or software that compresses or decompresses digital video, thus converting raw (uncompressed) digital video to a compressed format or vice versa. In the context of video compression, "codec" is a concatenation of "encoder" and "decoder"; a device that can only compress is typically called an encoder, and one that can only decompress is known as a decoder.

XML

XML, which stands for Extensible Markup Language, defines a set of rules for encoding documents in a format that is both human-readable and machine-readable.

XOR

See bitwise exclusive OR operation.

ZIP file format

An archive file format that supports lossless data compression. It is not a compression algorithm.

Index

Symbols

#PERFMATTERS, 79
7-Zip compression, 93

A

adaptive Huffman coding, 90
adaptive statistical encoding, 79-91
    adaptive arithmetic coding, 89-90
    adaptive Huffman coding, 90
    adaptive VLC encoding, 81-89
adaptive VLC encoding, 81-89
    decoding, 82
    dynamically building a VLC table, 81
    knowing when to reset, 88
    literals, 84
    real-world compression and, 89
    resets, 87
adjacency
    and contextuality, 151
    in delta coding, 116
    in dictionary transforms, 94
algorithms, data compression, 1
Amazon
    use of Markov chains, 139
    web page loading speed and conversion
        rates, 196
analog contexts, 152
ANS (see asymmetric numeral systems)
arithmetic coding, 60-69
    adaptive, 89-90
    decoding, 64
        improving performance of, 68
    encoding, 62
    finding the right number, 61

Huffman coding versus, 77
    origins of, 60
    picking the right output value, 64
    practical implementations, 69
ARJ archiver, 108
asymmetric numeral systems (ANS), 69-77
    creating the reference table, 71
    decoding example, 75
    encoding and decoding, using a transform
        table, 70
    source of the compression, 76
    using for compression, 74

B

base 10 number system, 9
base 2 number system, 10
base64-encoding PNG images in CSS files, 191
binary code, 45
binary number system, 10
binary numbers, 9
    converting from binary to decimal, 11
    converting from decimal to binary, 12
binary search, 14, 61
binary serialization formats, 186
binary trees (in Huffman encoding)
    building, 55
    setting up to generate codewords, 57
bits
    fixed-length buckets of bits for numbers, 17
    number required to represent numbers,
        LOG2 and, 17
bits-per-symbol (BPS) reset threshold, 88
bitwise exclusive OR (XOR) and delta coding,
    118

W

Walmart, web page loading speed and conversion rates, 196
WAV file format, 4
web page loading speed and conversion rates, 195
WebP image format, 177
  decompression performance and, 164
websites, increasing size of, 197
Weissman Score, 166
Weissman, Tsachy, 166
Welch, Terry, 109
Wheeler, David, 127
whole-word n-grams, 152
Witten, Ian, 146
words, finding the right words in dictionary transforms, 95

X

XML, 185
  converting from array-of-structs to struct-of-arrays, 188

human-readable text, 185
segmenting data into proper compression format, 191
slow decode times, 186
using binary serialization format instead of, 186
XOR delta coding, 118

Y

YouTube, 7
YouTube series, Compressor Head, 127

Z

zero-frequency problem, 150
Ziv, Jacob, 98
ZOO archiver, 109
ZPAQ algorithm, 153
  compression ratio and, 162
  decompression performance, 164
  memory use and running time, 153

About the Authors

Colt McAnlis is a developer advocate at Google focusing on games, compression, and performance. Before that, he was a graphics programmer in the games industry working at Blizzard, Microsoft (Ensemble), and Petroglyph. He's been an adjunct professor at SMU Guildhall, a UDACITY instructor (twice), and a book author. Recently, he's been teaching Android devs the zen of performance. When he's not working with developers, Colt spends his time preparing for an invasion of giant ants from outer space. He's also got a whole plethora of publications, videos, and other things, accounting for over 600,000 views.

Aleks Haecky is a developer advocate, training developer, and writer at Google with a passion for bridging the language gap between experts and their audience. He has worked behind the scenes of performance, Udacity, the Google Developer Channel, and documentation. In a previous life, he translated herpetological books and taught kayaking. Needless to say, he's also working on the next Great American Novel and lurks on LinkedIn.

Colophon

The animal on the cover of *Understanding Compression* is a Brazilian three-banded armadillo (*Tolypeutes tricinctus*).

This armadillo is indigenous to Brazil, as its name suggests. They live primarily in open savannahs and dry woodlands, preferring habitats with tall, woody grasses, scattered bushes, and gnarled trees. They are generally nocturnal, but have been known to forage during the day. They eat mainly ants and termites, which they find while shuffling along with their nose to the ground; they can smell prey through 20 cm of soil. Three-banded armadillos are great diggers, but they prefer to rest under bushes rather than in burrows. They do not rely on digging burrows for defense either, but instead roll into a ball and lock their armor. It is one of two species of armadillo that can roll into a ball.

Armadillos are usually solitary animals, but the three-banded armadillo occasionally travels in small families of up to three members. Mating season is October to January, with a brief courtship before mating. The gestation period lasts 120 days, resulting in a single, blind offspring. Newborn armadillo armor is soft, but its claws are fully developed and it can walk and roll into a ball within hours of birth. The Brazilian three-banded armadillo has undergone a 30% decrease in population in the last decade. Its only natural predators are adult pumas and jaguars, but its main threat is the destruction of its habitat to make room for livestock.

Many of the animals on O'Reilly covers are endangered; all of them are important to the world. To learn more about how you can help, go to *animals.oreilly.com*.

The cover image is from *Beeton's Dictionary*. The cover fonts are URW Typewriter and Guardian Sans. The text font is Adobe Minion Pro; the heading font is Adobe Myriad Condensed; and the code font is Dalton Maag's Ubuntu Mono.

Have it your way.

Get even more
for your money.

Join the O'Reilly Community, and register the O'Reilly books you own. It's free, and you'll get:

- $4.99 ebook upgrade offer
- 40% upgrade offer on O'Reilly print books
- Membership discounts on books and events
- Free lifetime updates to ebooks and videos
- Multiple ebook formats, DRM FREE
- Participation in the O'Reilly community
- Newsletters
- Account management
- 100% Satisfaction Guarantee

Signing up is easy:

1. Go to: oreilly.com/go/register
2. Create an O'Reilly login.
3. Provide your address.
4. Register your books.

Note: English-language books only

To order books online:
oreilly.com/store

For questions about products or an order:
orders@oreilly.com

To sign up to get topic-specific email announcements and/or news about upcoming books, conferences, special offers, and new technologies:
elists@oreilly.com

For technical questions about book content:
booktech@oreilly.com

To submit new book proposals to our editors:
proposals@oreilly.com

O'Reilly books are available in multiple DRM-free ebook formats. For more information:
oreilly.com/ebooks